FUTURE

English for Results

1

WORKBOOK with AUDIO CD

Margot Gramer

Series Consultants
Beatriz B. Diaz
Ronna Magy
Federico Salas-Isnardi

Future 1 Workbook with Audio CD
English for Results

Pearson Education, 10 Bank Street, White Plains, NY 10606

Staff credits: The people who made up the *Future 1 Workbook* team, representing editorial, production, design, and manufacturing, are Jennifer Adamec, Elizabeth Carlson, Aerin Csigay, Dave Dickey, Nancy Flaggman, Irene Frankel, Shelley Gazes, Michael Kemper, Melissa Leyva, and Barbara Sabella.

Cover design: Rhea Banker
Cover photo: Kathy Lamm/Getty Images
Text design: Barbara Sabella
Text composition: Rainbow Graphics
Text font: 13 pt Minion

Illustration credits: Steve Attoe: pp. 13, 29, 39, 75, 101 (top), 102, 120, 123; Luis Briseno: p. 103; Scott Fray: pp. 18, 76, 98; Brian Hughes: pp. 35, 63, 64, 96, 110, 112, 118; Stephen Hutchings: pp. 32 (top), 50, 60; Paul McCusker: pp. 15, 22, 41, 44, 101 (bottom), 122, 125; Steve Schulman: pp. 26, 27, 32 (bottom), 43, 65, 67, 82, 86, 105, 140; Anna Veltfort: p. 133

Photo Credits: All original photography by David Mager. Page 2 Digital Vision/Getty Images; 9(1) Bartomeu Amengual/age fotostock; 14(1) Kayte M. Deioma/PhotoEdit, (2) Frank Herholdt/Getty Images, (3) Stephe Simpson/Getty Images, (4) Royalty-Free Division/Masterfile, (5) Jim DeLillo/iStockphoto.com, (6) Index Stock Imagery, (7) Gary Crabbe/Alamy, (8) David De Lossy/Getty Images, (9) Photoshow/Dreamstime.com, 16(1) Blend Images/Alamy, (2) Royalty-Free Division/Masterfile, (3) Medioimages/Photodisc/Getty Images, (4) Frank Herholdt/Getty Images, (5) Corbis/Jupiterimages, (6) David Lewis/iStockphoto.com, (7) Shutterstock, (8) John Foxx/age fotostock; 21(1) Andersen Ross/age fotostock, (2) Thinkstock Images/Jupiterimages, (3) Gary Crabbe/Alamy, (4) Genevieve Engel/age fotostock, (5) wavebreakmedia/Shutterstock, (6) Dreamstime.com; 23 (right) Shutterstock; 24(1) Spencer Grant/PhotoEdit, (2) Jupiter Images/Comstock Images/Alamy, (3) Tetra Images/Jupiterimages, (4) Hongqi Zhang/123RF; 31 Shutterstock; 33(1) Shutterstock, (2) Shutterstock, (3) Felicia Martinez/PhotoEdit, (4) Tom Carter/PhotoEdit, (6) Shutterstock; 38 Tongro Image Stock/age fotostock; 40 Kevin Dodge/Masterfile; 55 Shutterstock, C Squared Studios/Getty Images, David Mager, David Mager, Photos.com/Jupiterimages; 62(1) Shutterstock, (2) Shutterstock, (3) Shutterstock, (4) Shutterstock, (5) Shutterstock, (6) Jupiterimages/Comstock Images/Alamy; 63(1) Shutterstock, (2) Shutterstock, (3) Echos/Jupiterimages, (4) Photos.com/Jupiterimages, (5) Shutterstock; 65(1a) Shutterstock, (1b) PNC/Getty Images, (2a) Shutterstock, (2b) Scott Van Dyke/Beateworks/Corbis, (4a) Dorling Kindersley, (4b) Rob Melnychuk/Getty Images; 80 Shutterstock; 86 Shutterstock; 88(1) Shutterstock, (2) Shutterstock, (3) Ingram Publishing/SuperStock, (4) Shutterstock, (5) Shutterstock, (6) Shutterstock; 89(1) Uyen Le/iStockphoto.com, (2) Shutterstock, (3) Shutterstock, (4) Shutterstock, (5) Barry Gregg/Corbis, (6) Shutterstock; 92(1) Shutterstock, Shutterstock, (2) Shutterstock, Shutterstock, (3) Shutterstock, Bobelias/Dreamstime.com, (4) Shutterstock, Shutterstock, (5) Shutterstock, Rachel Weill/Jupiterimages; 98(a) Sylvain Grandadam/Getty Images, (b) Keith Clarke/Fotolia.com, (c) Shutterstock, (d) Steve Dunwell/Index Stock Imagery; 99(1) Randy Faris/Corbis/Jupiterimages, (2) Tony Savino/The Image Works, (3) Christopher Allan/Getty Images, (4) Tara Donne/Getty Images; 103(a) AP Images, (b) Jim Zuckerman/Corbis, (c) David R. Frazier/PhotoEdit, (d) Najlah Feanny/Corbis, (e) Kent Wood/Photo Researchers, Inc., (f) AP Images, 107(L) Esbin-Anderson/age fotostock, (R) Edyta Linek/Fotolia.com; 108(1) Siede Preis/Getty Images, Shutterstock, (2) Shutterstock, (3) Steve Shott/Dorling Kindersley, Shutterstock, (4) Shutterstock, (5) Shutterstock, Shutterstock; 114(1) Shutterstock, (2) Shutterstock, (3) Art Stein/ZUMA/Corbis, (4) Shutterstock, (5) Shutterstock, (6) Shutterstock; 115(a) Shutterstock, (b) Image Farm Inc./Alamy, (c) Shutterstock, (d) Shutterstock, (e) Shutterstock; 124(1) Kathleen Finlay/Masterfile, (2) Guillermo Hung/Getty Images, (3) Ken Cavanagh/Photo Researchers, Inc., (4) Picture Partners/SuperStock; 129 Tom Grill/Corbis; 134(1) John Birdsall/age fotostock, (2) Thinkstock/Corbis, (3) Barros & Barros/Getty Images, (4) Andrew Woodley/Alamy, (5) Corbis/age fotostock, (6) Blend Images/Jupiterimages; 135(1) Tim Matsui/Alamy, (2) Lon C. Diehl/PhotoEdit, (3) Herjua/Fotolia, (4) Ann Marie Kurtz/iStockphoto.com; 137(1) Dmitry Kalinovsky/Shutterstock, (2) Gary Crabbe/Alamy, (3) Corbis/age fotostock, (4) Lon C. Diehl/PhotoEdit, (5) Pfutze/zefa/Corbis, (6) Tim Matsui/Alamy; 142(R) Photos.com/Jupiterimages.

ISBN-13: 978-0-13-199147-7
ISBN-10: 0-13-199147-7

Printed in the United States of America
20 17

Contents

To the Teacher

The *Future 1 Workbook with Audio CD* has 12-page units to complement what students have learned in the Student Book. Each Workbook unit follows the lesson order of the Student Book and provides supplemental practice in vocabulary, life skills, listening, grammar, reading, and writing. Students can complete the exercises outside the classroom as homework or during class time to extend instruction.

The Workbook Audio CD is a unique feature of the Workbook. It provides practice with conversations, grammar, and life skills competencies. In addition, the audio CD includes the readings from the Workbook so students can become more fluent readers.

UNIT STRUCTURE

Vocabulary
Practice focuses on the vocabulary presented on the first spread of the unit. Typical activities are word and sentence completion, labeling, and categorizing. Some lessons include sentence writing to reinforce the lesson's vocabulary, and some lessons include personalized exercises.

Grammar and Listening
Grammar is the main focus, with listening practiced as well. Grammar is practiced in contextualized exercises that include sentence completion, sentence writing, sentence scrambles, matching, and multiple choice. Listening activities include listening comprehension, listening dictation, and listening to check answers. Some lessons include vocabulary exercises to reinforce the new vocabulary taught in the lesson. Some lessons include personalized activities.

Life Skills
Realia-based exercises are featured on these pages, which also include vocabulary, grammar, listening, and personalized activities.

Life Skills Writing
The Life Skills Writing page extends the practice provided on the Life Skills Writing page found in the back of the Student Book. Students complete forms and other realia based on information provided or with personal information.

Reading
Each reading page includes a new reading related to the unit topic. Each reading is set up like a newspaper article, with a Greenville City News reporter asking a "person on the street" one or more questions. The reading is also on the audio CD so students can listen as they read. Each article is followed by a reading comprehension exercise and a personalized writing exercise.

ADDITIONAL RESOURCES

At the back of the Workbook, you will find:

- Audio Script
- Answer Key
- CD Track list
- Bound-in Audio CD

ORIENTATION

The Workbook, like the Student Book, includes an orientation for students. Before the students use the Workbook for the first time, direct them to To the Student on the next page. Go through the questions and tips with the students and answer any questions they may have so they can get the most out of using the Workbook.

To the Student

LEARN ABOUT YOUR BOOK

A PAIRS. Look in the back of your book. Find each section. Write the page number.

Audio Script ___ Answer Key ___ CD Track list ___

B PAIRS. Look at page 154. Find *Answers will vary.* What does *Answers will vary* mean?

C CLASS. Where is the Audio CD?

D CLASS. Look at page 5. What does [CD icon] mean? What does *Play Track 2* mean?

TIPS FOR USING THE AUDIO CD

CLASS. Read the tips for using the audio CD.

- For all exercises, listen to each track many times.
- For dictation exercises, use the pause button [pause icon] so you can have more time to write.
- After you finish the unit, for more listening practice, play the audio again and read the audio script in the back of the book at the same time.
- Also, for more listening practice, listen to the conversations and readings when you are in the car or on the bus.

WRITING TIPS

CLASS. Read the writing tips.

- Start sentences with a capital letter.
- End statements with a period (.).
- End questions with a question mark (?).

For example:

My name is Jack.

What's your name?

Unit 1: Getting to Know You

Lesson 1: Vocabulary

A **Complete the names of the countries.**

1. T_h_e U_n_i_t_ed S_t_at_e_s
2. M____i__o
3. __a__a__a
4. P__r__
5. H__it__
6. B__a__il
7. E__ S__l__a____r
8. E__g____nd
9. __o__an__
10. So__a____a
11. __h__na
12. K__re__
13. __us__i__
14. E__hi__pi__
15. __ie__n__m

B **Look at the map. Write the names of the countries that match the numbers. Use the countries in Exercise A.**

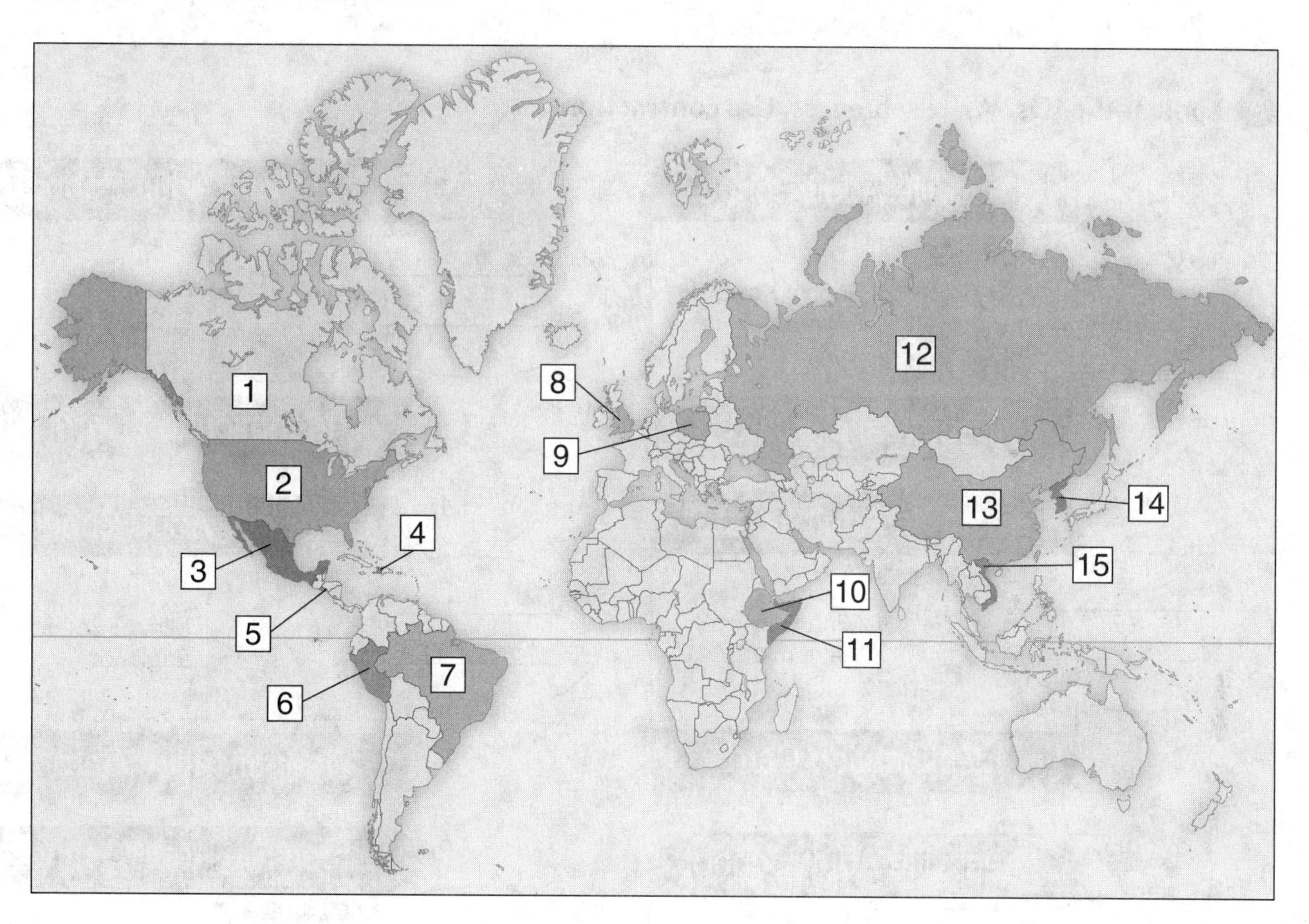

1. Canada ______
2. ______
3. ______
4. ______
5. ______
6. ______
7. ______
8. ______
9. ______
10. ______
11. ______
12. ______
13. ______
14. ______
15. ______

A **Look at the IDs. Write sentences. Use contractions.**

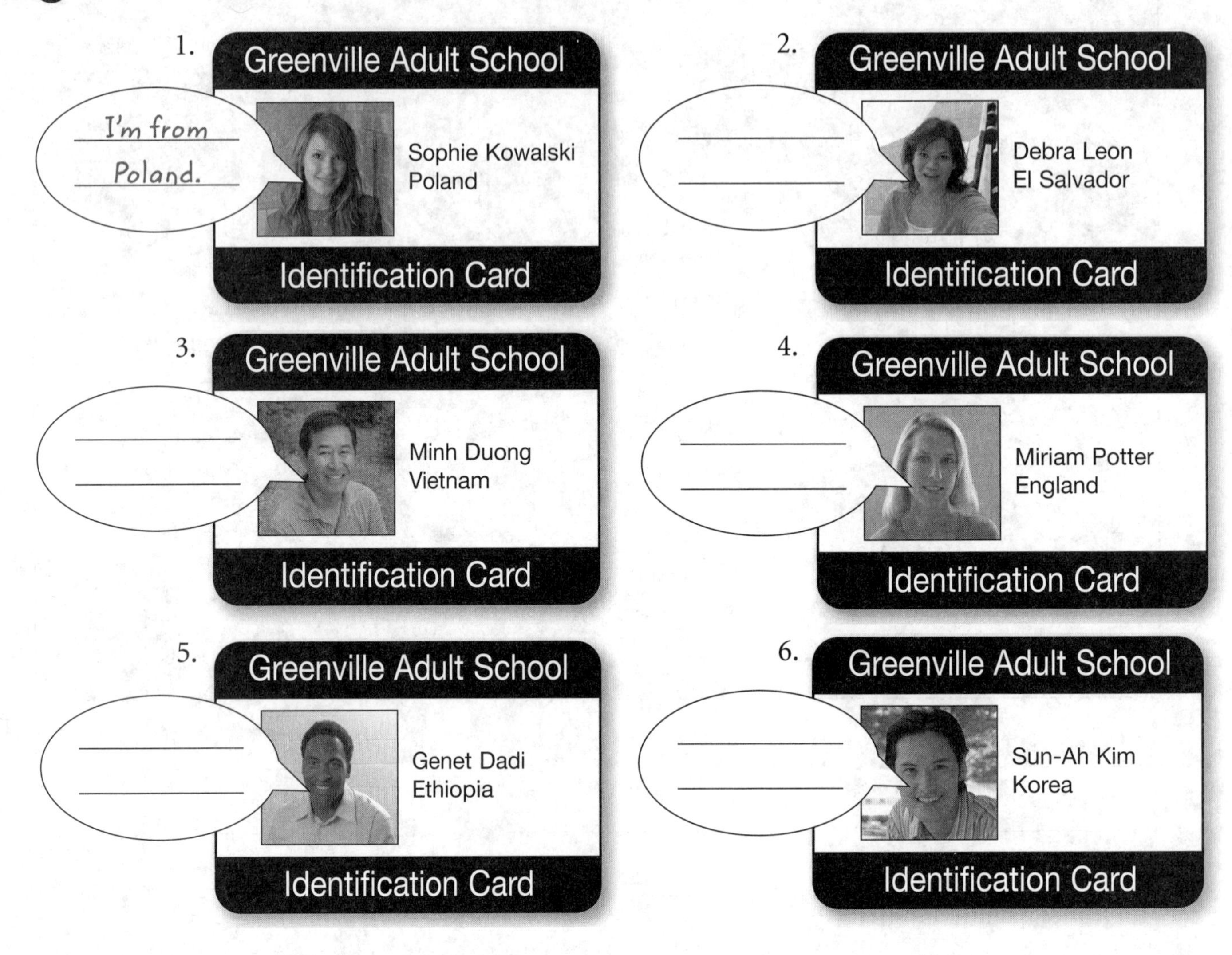

B **Look at the IDs in Exercise A. Complete the sentences.**

1. Sophie Kowalski is from Poland.
2. Debra Leon ______________________.
3. Minh Duong ______________________.
4. Miriam Potter ______________________.
5. Genet Dadi ______________________.
6. Sun-Ah Kim ______________________.

C **Put the conversation in the correct order. Write the correct numbers.**

____ Nice to meet you, too.

____ Hi, Marta. I'm Celia.

____ Nice to meet you, Celia.

____ Where are you from?

____ I'm from Brazil. What about you?

__1__ Hi, I'm Marta.

____ I'm from Peru.

D **Look at Exercise C. Write the conversation in the correct order.**

Marta: Hi, I'm Marta.

Celia: ____________________

Marta: ____________________

Celia: ____________________

Marta: ____________________

Celia: ____________________

Marta: ____________________

E **Play Track 2 to check your answers to Exercise D.**

F **Read the information and look at the pictures. Then answer the question.**

In the United States and Canada, people shake hands when they meet for the first time. What about in your country?

In my country, people ____________.

bow

hug

kiss

shake hands

Lesson 3: Say and spell your name

A Play Track 3. Listen to the conversations. Write the names you hear.

1. C a s a n d r a
2. ___ ___ ___ ___ ___ ___ ___
3. ___ ___ ___ ___ ___ ___ ___
4. ___ ___ ___ ___ ___ ___ ___
5. ___ ___ ___ ___ ___ ___
6. ___ ___ ___ ___ ___ ___ ___

B Play Track 4. Listen to the conversations. Complete the information cards.

1.

Mr. Mrs. Ms. Miss

First name: Allie

Last name: ____________

2.

Mr. Mrs. Ms. Miss

First name: ____________

Last name: ____________

3.

Mr. Mrs. Ms. Miss

First name: ____________

Last name: ____________

C **Put the names in alphabetical order. Write the names on the list.**

Antonio Vasquez
George Salder
Monica Briet
Sandra Montana
Yu-Min Lee
Jai-Soo Kim
Nyet Tran

Briet, Monica
____
____
____
____
____
____

> We sometimes write names in alphabetical order. We write the last name first. We put a comma after the last name:
>
> Chen, Martin
> Smith, Julie
> Young, Sarah

D **Put the names in alphabetical order. Write the names on the list.**

Chun-Mei Chong
Yao Chiang
Marta Conklin
Rafael Castillo
Moriz Cheban
Pedro Cardoso
Angela Colombo

Cardoso, Pedro
____
____
____
____
____
____

> When names start with the same letter, look at the second or third letter:
>
> Madison, Lynn
> Markinson, John
> Martine, Mark

E **Put the names in alphabetical order. Write the names on the list.**

Li Sun
Joel Rivera
Elaine Dols
Molly Abrams
Carla Mendez
Tania Ribeiro
Guy Monro

Abrams, Molly
____
____
____
____
____
____

Complete a personal information form

A **Read the conversation. Then complete the form.**

A: What's your name?

B: Bonita Marie Juevez.

A: How do you spell your first name, Ms. Juevez?

B: B-O-N-I-T-A.

A: How do you spell your last name?

B: J-U-E-V-E-Z.

Please print. Use blue or black ink.

Name: Juevez ______________________

LAST FIRST MIDDLE

☐ Male ☐ Female

Signature: Bonita Juevez ______________________

B **Complete the form. Use true or made-up information.**

Please print. Use blue or black ink. ☐ Male ☐ Female

Name:

_|_|_|_|_|_|_|_|_|_|_|_|_|_|_|_|_|_|_|_|_|_|_|_|_|_|_|_|_|_|_|_|_|_|_|_|_|_

LAST FIRST MIDDLE

Signature: ______________________

C **Unscramble the words to form sentences.**

1. My first name is Darya.
   (first / Darya / name / my / is)

2. ______________________
   (name / Ivanova / is / my / last)

3. ______________________
   (from / I'm / Ecuador)

4. ______________________
   (married / I'm)

A **Complete the sentences. Use *am* or *is*.**

1. I __am__ from Haiti. I ______ in level 2.
2. Sonya ______ from Russia. She ______ in level 1.
3. Jonas ______ from Poland. He ______ a student.

B **Rewrite the sentences. Replace the underlined words with *He* or *She*.**

1. Carla is from Peru.

She is from Peru.

2. Mr. Ruiz is from Mexico.

____

3. Mark is from the United States.

____

4. Jin-Su is from Korea.

____

C **Complete the conversations. Use pronouns and contractions.**

1. **A:** Where's Ms. Johnson from?
   B: __She's__ from Canada.
2. **A:** Where's Mr. Nowak from?
   B: ______ from Poland.
3. **A:** Where's Mrs. Nguyen from?
   B: ______ from Vietnam.
4. **A:** Where's Mr. Dias from?
   B: ______ from Brazil.

D **Rewrite the sentences in the negative. Then write another sentence. Use the words in parentheses. Use contractions.**

1. Katya is in level 2. (level 1) Katya isn't in level 2. She's in level 1.
2. José is from El Salvador. (Mexico) ____________________
3. She is from Canada. (Russia) ____________________
4. Mr. Fanelli is the teacher. (a student) ____________________
5. I am in level 3. (level 1) ____________________

E **Look at the list. Correct the sentences. Use *'s*, *is*, or *isn't*.**

Name	Country of Origin	Class
Ms. Cabral	Brazil	Level 3
Mr. Duval	Haiti	Level 1
Mrs. Gao	China	Level 1
Mr. Medina	Mexico	Level 2
Mr. Motalev	Russia	Level 3
Ms. Park	Korea	Level 2

1. Ms. Cabral is from China. Ms. Cabral isn't from China. She's from Brazil.
2. Mr. Duval is in Level 2. ____________________
3. Mrs. Gao is from Haiti. ____________________
4. Mr. Medina is from Brazil. ____________________
5. Mr. Motalev is in Level 2. ____________________
6. Ms. Park is in Level 3. ____________________

A Play Track 5. Listen and read.

THE GREENVILLE CITY NEWS

The Greenville City News reporter asks this question: *How is life in the United States?*

Ms. Park

I'm from Seoul, South Korea. Life in the United States is good. I have a nice apartment and a good job. I'm a student at Greenville Adult School. I'm in level 2. My family is here with me. We are very happy.

B Read the article again. Then read the sentences. Circle *True* or *False*.

1. Ms. Park is from Korea. (True) False
2. Ms. Park has a job. True False
3. Ms. Park is a student at Greenville Adult School. True False
4. Ms. Park is in level 1. True False
5. Ms. Park is not happy in the United States. True False

C Write about yourself. Complete the sentences.

I'm from ____________________, ____________________. I ____________

happy in the United States. I ____________ a student at ______________.

I'm in ______________________________.
(name of English class)

A **Complete the sentences. Use *is* or *are*. Then rewrite the sentences. Use contractions when possible.**

1. They ___are___ in level 2. ___They're in level 2.___
2. We ________ students. ____________________
3. You ________ a student. ____________________
4. Lev and I ________ from Russia. ____________________
5. Marta and Ilhan ________ in level 3. ____________________
6. It ________ interesting. ____________________

B **Unscramble the words to form sentences.**

1. ___We are from El Salvador.___
 (are / we / El Salvador / from)
2. ____________________
 (we / level 2 / in / are)
3. ____________________
 (Brazil / Tomas and Celia / from / are)
4. ____________________
 (are / a / you / student)
5. ____________________
 (Tania and I / today / absent / are)

C **Match the questions with the answers.**

1. Hi, what class are you in? ___d___
2. How's the class? ____
3. What about the students? ____
4. How's the teacher? ____

a. She's helpful.
b. They're great.
c. It's interesting.
d. We're in level 3.

D **Rewrite the sentences in the negative. Use contractions.**

1. They're in level 4. They aren't in level 4.
2. We're from Somalia. ____________________
3. My English class is hard. ____________________
4. Mr. and Mrs. Kim are from China. ____________________
5. Celia and I are students. ____________________
6. Calvin and Ricardo are from El Salvador. ____________________
7. Diego and Armando are students. ____________________
8. This book is interesting. ____________________

E **Play Track 6. Listen to the conversation. Write the missing words.**

Rob: Who's that?

Ana: That's the teacher.

Sue: That's __________ the teacher.

Ana: You're right. That's Mila.

Rob: Where's __________ from?

Ana: __________ from Russia. __________ in level 1.

Rob: Who's that?

Ana: That's Juan.

Sue: That's __________ Juan.

Ana: You're right. That's Mr. Jones.

Rob: Where's __________ from?

Ana: __________ from the United States. __________ the teacher. __________ great.

Unit 2: A Hard Day's Work

Lesson 1: Vocabulary

A **Complete the names of the jobs.**

1. s _a_ l _e_ s as _s_ ista _n_ t
2. g ___ r d ___ n ___ r
3. ___ o m ___ m a ___ e ___
4. a ___ t ___ s t
5. ___ r ___ v ___ r
6. n u ___ s ___
7. c ___ i l ___ - ___ a r ___ ___ o r ___ e r
8. d ___ c ___ o r
9. h ___ u s ___ k e ___ p ___ r

B **Look at the pictures. Write the jobs. Use the words in Exercise A.**

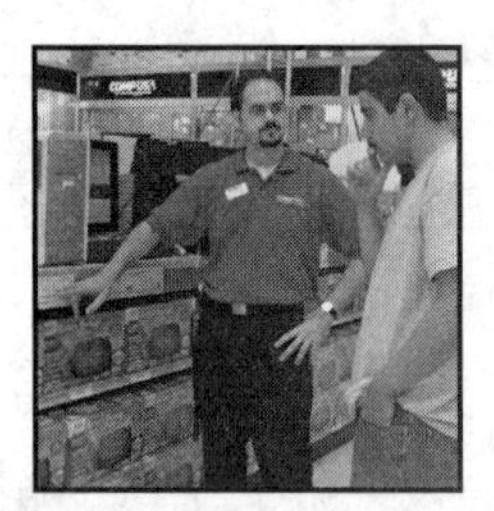

1. sales assistant

2. ____________

3. ____________

4. ____________

5. ____________

6. ____________

7. ____________

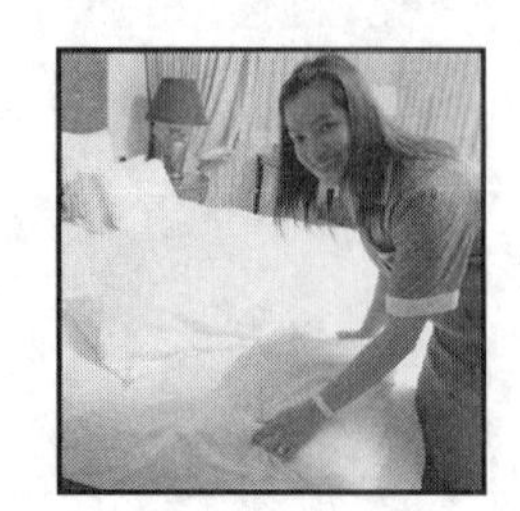

8. ____________

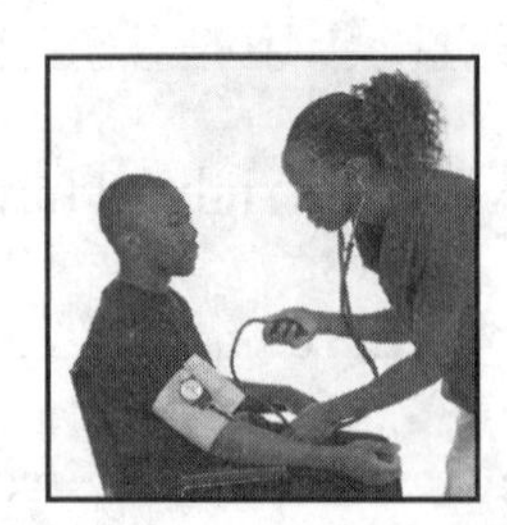

9. ____________

C **Look at the picture. Write the jobs of the people. Use the words in the box.**

cashier	cook	~~doctor~~	waitress

1. doctor
2. ______
3. ______
4. ______

D **Look at the picture. Write the jobs of the people. Use the words in the box.**

~~accountant~~	electrician	office assistant	painter

1. accountant
2. ______
3. ______
4. ______

A **Complete the sentences. Use *a* or *an*.**

1. Kim is __a__ cashier.

2. Yolanda is ____ artist.

3. Mario is ____ painter.

4. Beatriz is ____ driver.

5. Martin is ____ waiter.

6. Eva is ____ office assistant.

7. Alex is ____ cook.

8. Marisa is ____ accountant.

B **Combine the sentences.**

1. Paul is a doctor. Rafael is a doctor. Paul and Rafael are doctors.
2. Carla is a waitress. Lucia is a waitress. ______
3. Marco is a nurse. Tania is a nurse. ______
4. Liam is a gardener. Sal is a gardener. ______
5. Mia is an artist. Luz is an artist. ______
6. Kim is a cashier. Mike is a cashier. ______

C **Complete the conversation. Use the sentences in the box.**

I'm an office assistant. What about you?
~~Nice to meet you, too, Sonia.~~
Oh, that's interesting.

Mike: Sonia, this is Marie. Marie, this is Sonia.

Sonia: Hi, Marie. It's nice to meet you.

Marie: Nice to meet you, too, Sonia.

Sonia: So, Marie, what do you do?

Marie: ______

Sonia: I'm an office assistant, too.

Marie: ______

D **Play Track 7 to check your answers to Exercise C.**

A Play Track 8. Listen. Write the numbers.

0 1 2 ~~3~~ 4 5 6 7 8 9

1. 3 3. ____ 5. ____ 7. ____ 9. ____

2. ____ 4. ____ 6. ____ 8. ____ 10. ____

B Write the numbers in Exercise A in words.

1. three 3. ________ 5. ________ 7. ________ 9. ________

2. ________ 4. ________ 6. ________ 8. ________ 10. ________

C Play Track 9. Listen. Write the letter of the phone number you hear.

a.

b.

c.

d.

e.

1. d 2. ____ 3. ____ 4. ____ 5. ____

D **Write the phone numbers.**

1. (two-one-two) five-five-five-three-four-eight-zero (212)555-3480
2. (seven-one-eight) five-five-five-nine-three-two-two ____________
3. (six-three-one) five-five-five-one-eight-seven-one ____________
4. (nine-one-four) five-five-five-four-four-three-eight ____________

E **Play Track 10. Listen to the conversations. Complete the phone numbers.**

➤ Places of Interest in Mountainville

The Blue Moon Restaurant . . . .(473) 555-3 4 4 2

Kay's Clothes Store . . . .(473) 555-8____6

Mountainville Hospital . . . .(473) 555-___8___0

The Peamont Child-Care Center . . . .(473) 555-___7___8

Shelburn Office Supplies . . . .(473) 555-9____7

F **Play Track 11. Listen to the messages. Write the jobs and the phone numbers.**

1\. Call Mr. Lee about the waiter job at (_____) 555-_________.

2\. Call Monica Hempler about the ____________ job at (_____) 555-_________.

3\. Call Ms. Peterson about the ____________ job at (_____) 555-_________.

4\. Call Carlos Rivera about the ____________ job at (_____) 555-_________.

A **Read the conversation. Then complete the form.**

A: Your name please.

B: Monica Anne Chavez.

A: Can you spell your last name, please?

B: C-H-A-V-E-Z.

A: Is that Ms. or Mrs.?

B: Ms.

A: And your phone number?

B: (540) 555-8966.

A: Is that work or home?

B: Home. My work number is (498) 555-3200.
And my cell number is (783) 555-6521.

Title (please check)
Mr. ☐
Ms. ☐
Mrs. ☐
Miss ☐
Dr. ☐

Name (please print)

Chavez

LAST FIRST MIDDLE INITIAL

Phone Numbers

Home: ______________________

Work: ______________________

Cell: ______________________

B **Complete the form. Use true or made-up information.**

Name (please print)

____

LAST FIRST MIDDLE INITIAL

Title (please check)

Mr. ☐ Ms. ☐ Mrs. ☐ Miss ☐ Dr. ☐

Phone Numbers

Home: ______________________

Work: ______________________

Cell: ______________________

A **Complete the conversations. Use contractions when possible.**

1. A: ___Are___ you a teacher? B: Yes, I ___am___.
2. A: __________ he a painter? B: No, he __________.
3. A: __________ your job hard? B: No, it __________.
4. A: __________ they waiters? B: No, they __________.
5. A: __________ you a homemaker? B: No, I __________.

B **Look at the pictures. Write questions. Use the words in parentheses. Answer the questions with short answers. Use pronouns. Use contractions when possible.**

1. 

A: ___Is Rob an electrician?___
(Rob / electrician)
B: ___Yes, he is.___

2. 

A: __________
(Sara and Ann / artists)
B: __________

3. 

A: __________
(Mr. Ruiz / gardener)
B: __________

4. 

A: __________
(Carl and Miguel / cooks)
B: __________

5. 

A: __________
(Jason / accountant)
B: __________

6. 

A: __________
(Bianca and Sam / doctors)
B: __________

C Play Track 12. Listen to the conversations. Write the correct occupation for each person.

D Look at Exercise C. Complete the conversations. Write a question and short answer. Use the names in parentheses. Use contractions when possible.

1. **A:** That's Hong-Yi. He's an electrician.

   B: (Rodrigo) Is Rodrigo an electrician, too?

   A: No, he isn't. He's an artist.

2. **A:** That's Kim. She's a child-care worker.

   B: (Ms. Torres) ____________________, too?

   A: ____________________

3. **A:** That's Calvin. He's a cook.

   B: (Robert) ____________________, too?

   A: ____________________

4. **A:** That's Daniel. He's an office assistant.

   B: (Elena / Kristina) ____________________, too?

   A: ____________________

A Play Track 13. Listen and read.

THE GREENVILLE CITY NEWS

The Greenville City News reporter asks this question: *What do you do?*

Nina Popova

I'm a student at Greenville Adult School. And I'm also a sales assistant at Computer World in Bayville.

John Bernard

I'm an accountant at Bannon Accounting in New York. I love my job.

Pavlic Chebakov

I'm a student at Hunter College. My classes are interesting. And I'm also a cashier at Tony's Restaurant in Middletown.

B **Read the article again. Then answer the questions. Write sentences.**

1. Is Nina Popova an accountant? No, she isn't.
2. Is she a student? __________
3. Is John Bernard a sales assistant? __________
4. Is he a student? __________
5. Is Pavlic Chebakov a cashier? __________
6. Is he a student? __________

C **Write about yourself. Complete the sentences. Use the responses above as a model.**

My name is __________. I'm a student at __________. I'm also a/an __________.

A **Complete the sentences. Use *work* or *works*. Then match the jobs with the places.**

1. I ___work___ at a school. _c_
2. They ________ at a construction site. ____
3. Joe ________ at a factory. ____
4. Grace and Lucille ________ at a store. ____
5. He ________ at a nursing home. ____

a. stock clerks
b. an assembly-line worker
c. a teacher
d. a caregiver
e. carpenters

B **Complete the sentences. Use *work* or *works*.**

1. I ___work___ at a restaurant.
2. He ________ at a school.
3. We ________ in New York.
4. They ________ in Los Angeles.
5. Ms. Benito ________ at an office.
6. Dr. Yu ________ at a hospital.

C **Play Track 14. Listen to the sentences. Match the sentences with the pictures.**

1. ____

2. ____

3. _a_

4. ____

D **Complete the sentences. Use the correct form of the verbs in parentheses.**

1. My husband and I ___are___ (be) from Cuba. We ________ (live) in Miami. My husband ________ (work) at a hospital. I ________ (work) at a bank.
2. Carlos ________ (be) a caregiver. He ________ (work) at a nursing home. He ________ (live) in Dallas.
3. Martin and Tomacz ________ (live) in San Diego. They ________ (be) accountants. They ________ (work) at an accounting office.

E **Complete the conversation. Use the sentences in the box.**

Are you a student here?	~~Hi, I'm Edna.~~
I work in Boston.	I'm an artist.
It's nice to meet you.	Really? That's interesting.

Edna: ___Hi, I'm Edna.___

Sam: Hi, Edna. I'm Sam.

Edna: ________________________

Sam: It's nice to meet you, too.

Edna: ________________________

Sam: No, I'm not. I'm a teacher.

Edna: ________________________

Sam: What do you do, Edna?

Edna: ________________________

Sam: Really? Where do you work?

Edna: ________________________

Sam: That's great!

F **Play Track 15 to check your answers to Exercise E.**

Unit 3: Time for Class

Lesson 1: Vocabulary

A **Look at the picture. Write the names of the things that match the numbers. Use the words in the box.**

backpack	~~board~~	book	cell phone
chair	chalk	computer	desk

1. board
2. ____________
3. ____________
4. ____________
5. ____________
6. ____________
7. ____________
8. ____________

B **Look at the desk. Write the names of the things that match the numbers. Use the words in the box.**

CD	dictionary	eraser	folder
marker	notebook	~~piece of paper~~	three-ring binder

1. piece of paper
2. ______
3. ______
4. ______
5. ______
6. ______
7. ______
8. ______

C **Look at Exercise B. Complete the conversations about the things in the picture. Use *on the desk* or *in the backpack*.**

1. **A:** Where's my eraser?

   B: It's on the desk.

2. **A:** Where's my binder?

   B: It's ______.

3. **A:** Where's my folder?

   B: It's ______.

4. **A:** Where's my dictionary?

   B: It's ______.

5. **A:** Where's my notebook?

   B: It's ______.

A **Complete the sentences. Use the words in the box.**

listen	try to	turn off	~~write~~

1. Write in your notebooks.
2. ________ to your teacher.
3. ________ your cell phone.
4. ________ come to class on time.

B **Rewrite the sentences in the negative. Use contractions.**

1. Look at the book.
   Don't look at the book.
2. Write your name.
   ____
3. Open your dictionary.
   ____
4. Take out your notebook.
   ____
5. Use a pencil.
   ____
6. Bring your book.
   ____

C **Look at the pictures. Match the sentences with the pictures. Write one sentence from the box under each picture.**

Don't eat in class.	Don't take out your notebook.
~~Don't use a pen.~~	Look at the picture.
Take out your book.	Use a pencil.

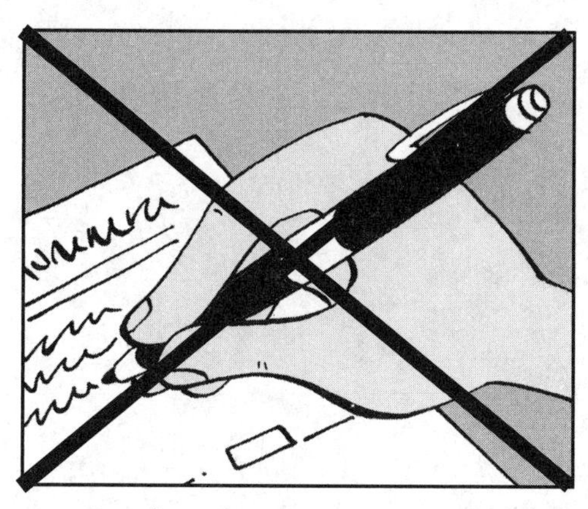

1. Don't use a pen.

2. ______________________

3. ______________________

4. ______________________

5. ______________________

6. ______________________

Complete a school registration form

A **Read the conversation. Then complete the school registration form.**

A: What's your name, please?

B: Paulo Brito.

A: What's your phone number?

B: It's (385) 555-1497.

A: OK. What class are you in?

B: English 2. Who's the teacher?

A: The teacher is Mr. Franklin.

B: What classroom is that?

A: It's Room 312.

B: Thank you.

Student's Name: Paulo ____________________ ☐ M
FIRST LAST ☐ F

Phone: ____________________

Subject: ____________________

Teacher: ____________________

Classroom: ____________________

B **Complete the form. Use true or made-up information.**

☐ M
☐ F

Student's Name: ____________________
FIRST LAST

Phone: ____________________

Subject: ____________________

Teacher: ____________________

Classroom: ____________________

A  **Play Track 16. Listen and read.**

THE GREENVILLE CITY NEWS

The Greenville City News reporter asks this question: *What are the rules in your English class?*

Martin Wu

I'm a student at Greenville Adult School. I'm in level 1. Here are five rules in my English class:

1. Try to come on time.
2. Listen to the teacher.
3. Don't interrupt your classmates.
4. Bring your book, a notebook, and a pen or pencil.
5. Don't answer your cell phone in class.

B Read the article again. Which rules are correct? Circle *True* or *False*.

1. Try to come on time.	(True)	False
2. Listen to the teacher.	True	False
3. Interrupt your classmates.	True	False
4. Bring your book, a notebook, and a cell phone to class.	True	False
5. Answer your cell phone in class.	True	False

C Look at the rules in Exercise A. Can you think of another rule? Write the rule. Use Martin Wu's response as a model.

____

____

A **Look at the pictures. Complete the sentences. Use *This, That, These,* or *Those.***

1. ___This___ is a great mouse.
2. ___________ are my pens.

3. ___________ are good markers.
4. ___________ is a great computer.

B **Rewrite the sentences. Change the sentences to the plural.**

1. That's a great backpack. ___Those are great backpacks.___
2. This is a good marker. ___________
3. That's my book. ___________
4. This is a great keyboard. ___________
5. This is my binder. ___________
6. That's a good dictionary. ___________

C **Look at the pictures. Complete the sentences. Use *This, That, These,* or *Those* and *is* or *are.***

1. 

___That is___ your ___computer___.

2. 

___________ great ___________.

3. 

___________ my ___________.

4. 

___________ great ___________.

D Play Track 17. Look at the pictures. Listen to the questions. Write the questions and answers. Use contractions when possible.

1. A: Is this a monitor?
   B: Yes, it is.
2. A: ______
   B: ______
3. A: ______
   B: ______
4. A: ______
   B: ______
5. A: ______
   B: ______
6. A: ______
   B: ______

E Answer the questions. Circle the letter of the correct answer.

1. What's this called in English?
   a. These are desks. b. They're desks. (c.) It's a desk.
2. What's that called in English?
   a. It's a keyboard. b. Those are keyboards. c. This is a keyboard.
3. What are these called in English?
   a. That's a CD. b. Those are CDs. c. They're CDs.
4. What are those called in English?
   a. That's a DVD. b. They're DVDs. c. It's a DVD.
5. Is this a mouse?
   a. Yes, they are. b. Yes, this is. c. Yes, it is.
6. Is that a monitor?
   a. Yes, it is. b. Yes, this is. c. Yes, they are.
7. Are those new folders?
   a. Yes, those are. b. Yes, they are. c. Yes, it is.

A **Put the numbers in the box in the correct order.**

46 ~~18~~ 74 89 62 ~~23~~ 97 58 100 35

1. 18
2. 23
3. ___
4. ___
5. ___
6. ___
7. ___
8. ___
9. ___
10. ___

B **Look at the numbers. Write the words.**

1. 25 twenty-five
2. 42 ___
3. 14 ___
4. 84 ___
5. 71 ___
6. 60 ___
7. 36 ___
8. 100 ___

C **Play Track 18. Listen to the conversations. Complete the directory.**

Directory

Cafeteria 17

Computer Lab .... ___

Library .... ___

Main Office .... ___

D **Look at the floor plan. Then complete the conversations about the building.**

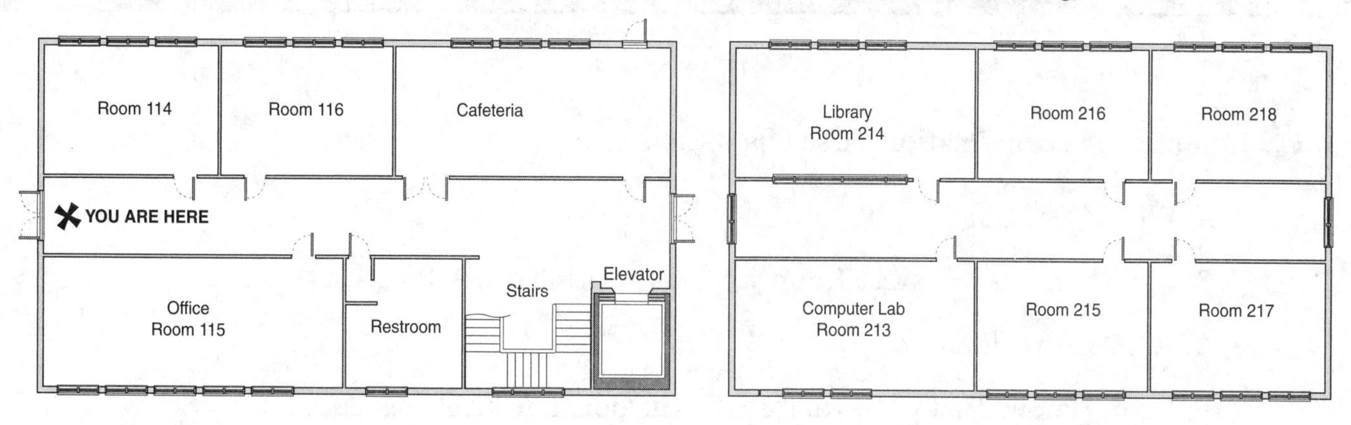

1. **A:** Excuse me. Which way is the restroom?

   B: It's down the hall on the right, across from the cafeteria.

2. **A:** Which way is ____________________?

   B: It's down the hall on the left, across from the stairs.

3. **A:** Which way is ____________________?

   B: It's across from the office, next to Room 116.

4. **A:** Which way is ____________________?

   B: It's upstairs, Room 213. It's across from the library.

5. **A:** Which way is ____________________?

   B: It's upstairs next to the library.

6. **A:** Which way is ____________________?

   B: It's upstairs, across from Room 216.

E **Look at the floor plan in Exercise D. Answer the questions. Use the words in parentheses.**

1. Where's Room 218? It's across from Room 217.
   (**across from**)
2. Where's the library? ____________________
   (**next to**)
3. Where's Room 114? ____________________
   (**across from**)
4. Where's the cafeteria? ____________________
   (**next to**)
5. Where's the elevator? ____________________
   (**across from**)

A **Complete the conversations. Use *him* or *her*.**

1. **A:** Where's the office?
   B: I don't know. That's Ms. Kramer. She's the principal. Ask ___her___.
2. **A:** Where's the elevator?
   B: I don't know. That's Mr. Yu. He's the custodian. Ask ________.
3. **A:** Is the library upstairs?
   B: I don't know. That's Mrs. Cowalski. She's the librarian. Ask ________.
4. **A:** Is the computer lab open?
   B: I don't know. That's Paulo. He's the computer lab assistant. Ask ________.
5. **A:** Where's the ESL office?
   B: I don't know. That's Miss White. She's the office assistant. Ask ________.

B **Play Track 19 to check your answers to Exercise A.**

C **Rewrite the sentences. Change the underlined word or words to *him*, *her*, *it*, or *them*.**

1. Please call <u>Rosa</u>. ___Please call her.___
2. Don't open <u>the book</u>. ________
3. Please help <u>Ramon and Silvia</u>. ________
4. How do you spell <u>your name</u>? ________
5. Call <u>Ms. Heiden</u> about the job. ________
6. Ask <u>Mr. Duval</u> for help. ________

D **Complete the sentences. Use *me, him, her, us, them, you,* or *it*.**

1. I'm at home today. Please call ___me___.
2. Marco is talking. Please don't interrupt ________.
3. Please close your books. Don't use ________ now.
4. Ms. Santos is our teacher. We like ________.
5. We're new students. We have a question. Can you help ________?
6. The students are absent. Can you call ________?
7. The book is interesting. Read ________.
8. They're new students. Please talk to ________.
9. Are you the office assistant? Can I ask ________ a question?
10. We don't understand. Please help ________.

E **Complete the conversation. Use the sentences in the box.**

~~Can you help me?~~	It's down the hall on the left, Room 24.
That's Mr. Smith, the custodian.	What room is the ESL office?

Bob: Excuse me. ___Can you help me?___

Meg: Sure.

Bob: ________________

Meg: Sorry. I don't know. Ask him.

Bob: Uh . . . who's he?

Meg: ________________

Bob: Excuse me. Which way is the ESL office?

Mr. Smith: ________________

Bob: Thank you.

Mr. Smith: You're welcome.

F **Play Track 20 to check your answers to Exercise E.**

Unit 4: Family Ties

Lesson 1: Vocabulary

A **Complete the family words.**

1. p__a__r__e__n__t__s
2. d___ug___t___r
3. c___i___dr___n
4. ___if___
5. ___on
6. gr___n___m___t___er
7. hu___b___n___
8. s___st___r
9. ___o___he___
10. b___ot___e___
11. g___a___df___t___e___
12. f___t______r

B **Complete the chart. Write the family words in the correct column.**

Male	Female	Male and Female
father	mother	parents
	daughter	
	grandmother	
brother		
husband		

C **Look at Robert's family. Write sentences with *he, she,* and *they.* Use the words in the box. Use contractions.**

children daughter father mother ~~parents~~ son wife

1. They're Robert's parents.
2. ______________________
3. ______________________
4. ______________________
5. ______________________
6. ______________________
7. ______________________

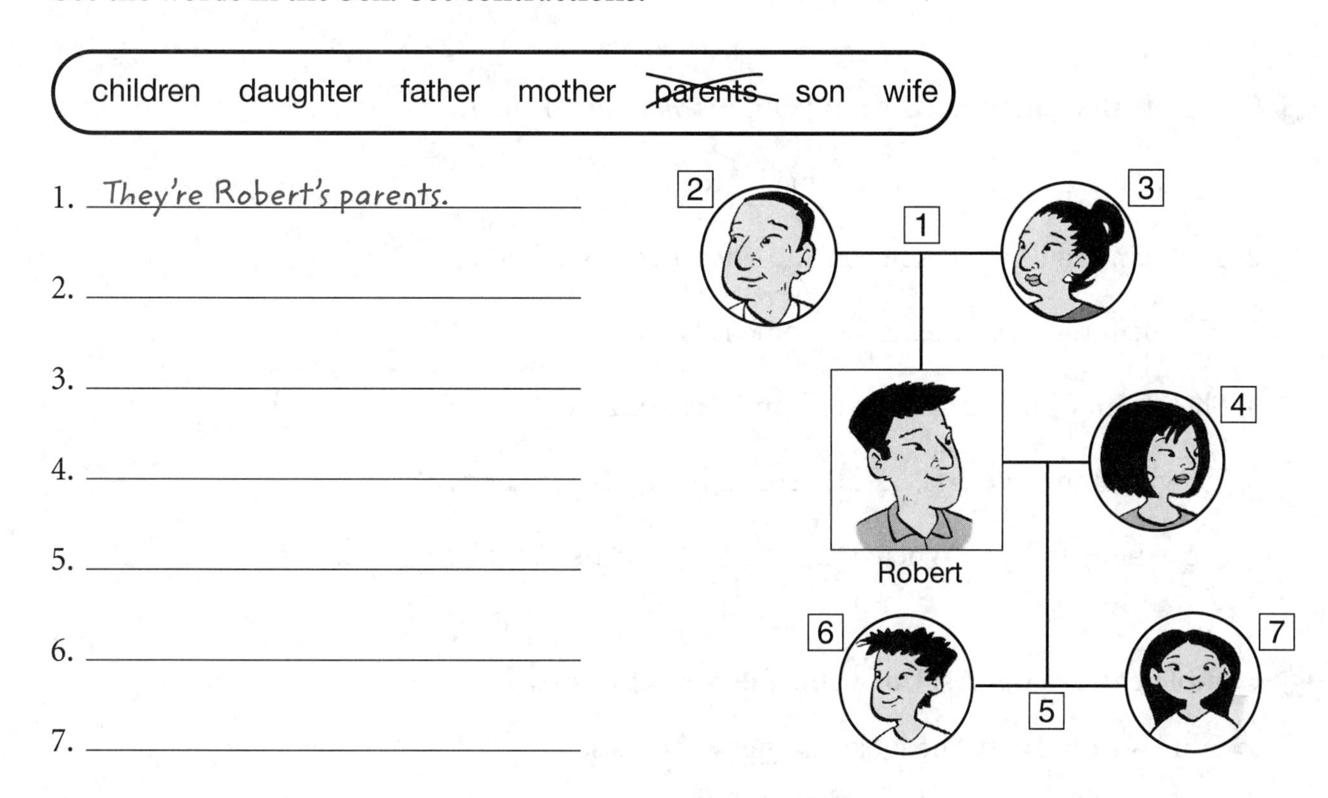

D **Look at the pictures. Complete the sentences about the people in Robert's family. Use contractions.**

A **Complete the sentences. Use *my, your, his, her, our,* or *their.***

1. I'm Jack. ___My___ last name is Hoyt.
2. You're in English 201. __________ teacher is Ms. Rado.
3. He's Benny. __________ last name is Hart.
4. She's from Chile. __________ family is in Miami.
5. They're in the cafeteria. __________ backpacks are here.
6. We're new students. Where is __________ classroom?

B **Complete the sentences. Underline the correct words.**

1. Edna is from Haiti. She looks like **her** / **their** sister.
2. Ivan and Oleg are brothers. **Their** / **His** parents are in Russia.
3. Marisa and **his** / **her** husband live in Brazil, but **his** / **their** children live in Los Angeles.
4. We're waiters. The restaurant is across from **his** / **our** house.
5. Felix looks like **their** / **his** sister. They live with **our** / **their** parents.
6. Carlos and I are students. **Their** / **Our** class is in Room 230.

C **Complete the paragraph. Write the correct possessive adjectives.**

This is a picture of ___my___ (1. **my / your**) aunt and uncle, and these are __________ (2. **our / their**) children. Silvia looks like __________ (3. **his / her**) mother. Francisco looks like __________ (4. **his / her**) father. And Antonio looks like __________ (5. **our / his**) father and __________ (6. **his / her**) mother.

D **Look at Jack's family tree. Complete the sentences.**

1. **A:** Who's Molly?

   B: She's ___Jack's___ cousin.

2. **A:** Who's Monique?

   B: She's __________ wife.

3. **A:** Who's Stanley?

   B: He's __________ husband.

4. **A:** Who's Marie?

   B: She's __________ mother.

5. **A:** Who's Frank?

   B: He's __________ brother.

Stanley Monique Uncle Frank Aunt Marie

Jack Molly

E **Complete the conversation. Use the sentences in the box.**

Fran looks like her.	He looks like your mother, too.
She looks nice. Is that your mother?	~~That's my sister, Fran.~~

Eva: That's a great photo. Who's that?

Tom: ___That's my sister, Fran.___

Eva: ______________________________

Tom: Yes, it is.

Eva: ______________________________

Tom: Yes. And this is my brother, Tim.

Eva: ______________________________

Tom: I know. And I look like my father.

F **Play Track 21 to check your answers to Exercise E.**

A Play Track 22. Listen and read.

THE GREENVILLE CITY NEWS

The Greenville City News reporter asks this question:
Is your family here in the U.S.?

Min-Ji Nowak

My mother and father are in Korea, but I live in New York with my husband, Tom, and our daughter, Lily. My sister and her husband live in New York, too. They have two sons. My brother lives in California. He's not married. I have an aunt and uncle here, too. They live in New Jersey. So, I have family here, and in Korea.

B **Read the article again. Then complete the sentences. Circle the letter of the correct answer.**

1. Min-Ji _____ family in this country.	(a) has	b. doesn't have
2. Her _____ are in Korea.	a. brothers	b. parents
3. She lives with her _____.	a. brother	b. husband and daughter
4. They live in _____.	a. New Jersey	b. New York
5. Her _____ has two sons.	a. sister	b. brother
6. Her _____ has two cousins.	a. daughter	b. husband
7. Her _____ lives in California.	a. brother	b. sister
8. Her aunt and uncle live in _____.	a. New Jersey	b. New York

C **Are your family and friends in the U.S.? Write sentences. Use Min-Ji's response as a model.**

____

____

____

A **Complete the sentences. Use *am, is, are, have,* or *has.***

1. Enrique ___has___ a beard.
2. Mia ________ average height.
3. You aren't heavy. You ________ thin.
4. I ________ short and thin. I ________ short hair.
5. Sue ________ tall and thin. She ________ long hair.
6. Bill ________ heavy, and he ________ a mustache.
7. Tom and Pat ________ brothers. They both ________ long hair.

B **Complete the sentences. Use contractions when possible.**

1. She ___'s___ short. She ___has___ short hair.
2. He ________ a beard. He ________ tall.
3. He ________ short. He ________ a mustache.
4. She ________ tall. She ________ long hair.
5. He ________ heavy. He ________ short hair.

C **Look at Exercise B. Match the pictures with the sentences. Write the number of the correct sentence.**

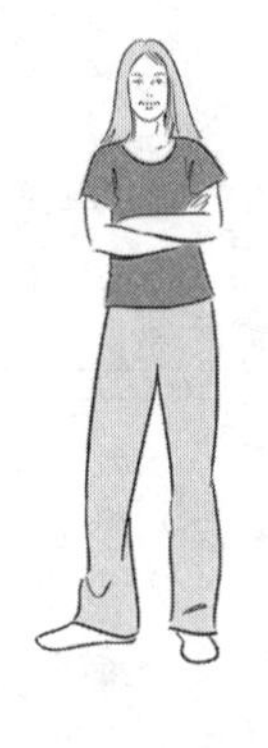
______

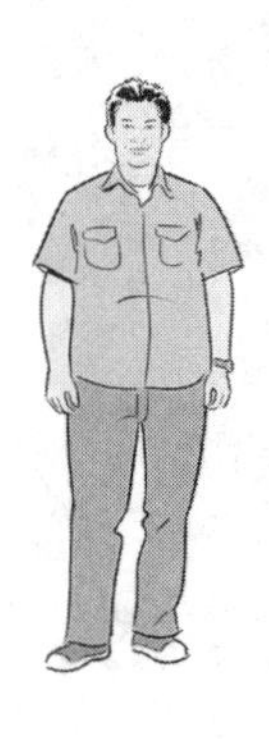
______

______

___1___

______

D **Look at the picture. Describe the people. Write sentences.**

1. Philip is short and average weight. He has short hair.

2. ______________________________

3. ______________________________

E **Complete the conversation. Use the sentences in the box.**

Does he look like you?	Does she look like you?
~~Is your family here in this country?~~	What's your brother like?

Mary: Is your family here in this country?

Luz: Well, my brother and sister are here. My parents are in Mexico.

Mary: ______________________________

Luz: He's great.

Mary: ______________________________

Luz: Yes. He's tall and thin and has short hair.

Mary: What about your sister? ______________________________

Luz: No. She's average height and heavy. She has long hair.

F **Play Track 23 to check your answers to Exercise E.**

A Play Track 24. Look at the calendar. Listen to the conversation. Circle the dates you hear. Write the information on the calendar. Use the words in the box.

~~Judy's birthday~~ Kevin's birthday Randy's birthday Martha's birthday James's birthday

FEBRUARY

Sunday	Monday	Tuesday	Wednesday	Thursday	Friday	Saturday
1	2	3	4	(5) Judy's birthday	6	7
8	9	10	11	12	13	14
15	16	17	18	19	20	21
22	23	24	25	26	27	28

B Look at the dates in Exercise A. Write sentences.

1. Judy's birthday is February 5.
2. ______
3. ______
4. ______
5. ______

C **Look at the ID cards. Write the dates of birth.**

Name: Elsa Torres

DOB: 3-18-75

Name: Robert Sinclair

DOB: 8-30-45

1. March 18, 1975
2. ______________________

Name: Hin-Shi Suk

DOB: 11-29-85

Name: Simone Chantall

DOB: 2-17-69

3. ______________________
4. ______________________

Name: Roberto Soto

DOB: 5-22-81

Name: Pavlina Ivanova

DOB: 12-21-84

5. ______________________
6. ______________________

D **Play Track 25. Listen. Write the dates in numbers.**

1. 5-4-04
2. __________
3. __________
4. __________
5. __________
6. __________
7. __________
8. __________

A **Complete the conversations. Use *is* or *are* and a pronoun, if necessary. Use contractions when possible.**

1. **A:** How old ___is___ your son?

   B: ___He's___ 12.

2. **A:** How old ________ your kids?

   B: Well, Zoey ________ two and Brandon ________ eight months.

3. **A:** How old ________ your brother?

   B: ________ 23.

4. **A:** How old ________ your grandchildren?

   B: ________ seven and five.

5. **A:** How old ________ Steven's sister?

   B: I don't know. I think ________ around 30.

B **Play Track 26. Listen to the conversation. Complete the ages and grades of the children on the form.**

Holt Central School District

Parents

Father: Hernandez, Martin **Mother:** Hernandez, Anna

Children	Age	Grade
José	____	____
Carmen	____	____
Miguel	____	____

C **Read the paragraph about Mike and his sister and brother.**

> Mike is 10 years old. He's in the fifth grade. He is thin. He has long hair. His sister, Christine, is 13. She's in the eighth grade. She's average weight and height. She has short hair. His brother, Brian, is 15. He's in the ninth grade. He's thin and average height. He has long hair.

D **Complete the questions and answers about Mike and his sister and brother. Use contractions when possible.**

1. ___How old is___ Mike? ___He's___ 10 ___years old___.
2. ___Is he in___ the fourth grade? No, ___he isn't. He's in the fifth grade___.
3. ______________ Mike's sister? ________ 13 ______________.
4. ______________ the eighth grade? Yes, ______________.
5. ______________ Mike's brother? ________ 15 ______________.
6. ______________ the tenth grade? No, ______________.

E **Complete the conversation. Use the sentences in the box.**

And her son is seven.	How old are they?
~~I'm at my cousin's house.~~	She's in the fourth grade.

Mark: Hi, Nina. Where are you?

Nina: ___I'm at my cousin's house.___ I'm babysitting for her kids.

Mark: Oh, that's nice. ______________

Nina: Well, her daughter is nine. ______________

______________ He's in the second grade.

F **Play Track 27 to check your answers to Exercise E.**

Complete an emergency contact form

A **Look at the note. Then complete the emergency contact form for Sandra Escovar.**

In case of emergency

Call my husband Carlos
Work (days): (498) 555-2221
Home (nights): (498) 555-2379
Cell: (495) 555-3696

Call my mother, Monica Ortiz
Home (days): (674) 555-9876

Emergency Contact Information

Name: ______________________, ______________________
(last) (first)

In case of emergency, call:

Name	Relationship	Daytime Phone	Evening Phone	Other Phone
Carlos Escovar				
			—	—

B **Complete the emergency contact form. Use true or made-up information.**

Emergency Contact Information

Name (last) ______________________ (first) ______________________

In case of emergency, call:

Name	Relationship	Daytime Phone	Evening Phone	Other Phone

Unit 5: Shop, Shop, Shop

Lesson 1: Vocabulary

A **Look at the pictures. Write the clothing items you see. Use the words in the box. Add *a* when necessary. Some words are used more than once.**

blouse	dress	jacket	jeans	pants	shirt
shoes	skirt	sneakers	socks	sweater	T-shirt

1. a dress
   shoes

2. ______
   ______
   ______

3. ______
   ______
   ______

4. ______
   ______
   ______

5. ______
   ______
   ______

6. ______
   ______
   ______

B **Look at the clothing items in Exercise A. Write the words in the correct column.**

Singular		Plural	
a dress	______	socks	______
______	______	______	______
______	______	______	
______			

C **Write new sentences. Use *It's* or *They're*.**

1. The shirt is yellow. It's a yellow shirt.
2. The socks are black. They're black socks.
3. The dress is pink. ______
4. The sneakers are red. ______
5. The jacket is purple. ______
6. The pants are beige. ______

D **Look at the picture on page 101 in your Student Book. Complete the sentences. Write the correct colors.**

1. The customer is wearing a yellow sweater and ______ pants.
2. She is wearing ______ shoes.
3. She is returning a ______ shirt.

E **What are *you* wearing? Write the clothes and colors. Use the example below as a model.**

I'm wearing a blue shirt and black pants. I'm wearing black shoes and gray socks.

______

______

A Complete the sentences. Underline *need* or *needs*.

1. Jack **need** / **needs** a new jacket.
2. Sun-Li **need** / **needs** a new dress.
3. Sam and Harry **need** / **needs** new sneakers.
4. I **need** / **needs** a new wallet.
5. We **need** / **needs** new T-shirts.
6. My brother **need** / **needs** new shoes.
7. They **need** / **needs** new pants.
8. You **need** / **needs** a new jacket.

B Write sentences. Use the words in parentheses and *has* or *have*.

1. (Carla / a new watch) Carla has a new watch.
2. (Alex and Sufia / black pants) ______
3. (I / new shoes) ______
4. (Matthew / a new sweater and jeans) ______
5. (We / new blouses) ______
6. (Eric / a yellow backpack) ______
7. (Luis and Mark / new sneakers) ______
8. (You / a brown jacket) ______
9. (We / new shirts) ______
10. (Mr. Lee / black shoes) ______

C Look at the lists. What does each person want? Write sentences.

Ricardo	Sarah & Tina	Carl	Thomas and Ivan
backpack	blouse	jacket	T-shirt
sneakers	skirt	pants	watch

1. Ricardo wants a new backpack and sneakers.
2. ______________________
3. ______________________
4. ______________________

D Complete the sentences. Use the correct form of the verbs in parentheses.

1. Ya-Wen wants (want) a new shirt and jeans.
2. Danny ________ (need) new sneakers.
3. Chi ________ (have) a new shirt.
4. Tania and Monika ________ (want) new skirts.
5. We ________ (need) new jackets.
6. I ________ (have) a new handbag.
7. Ben ________ (need) new socks.
8. My daughters ________ (have) new jeans.
9. Paulo and Brian ________ (want) new wallets.
10. Ms. Lee ________ (have) a new dress.

E What clothes do you want? Complete the sentence.

I ______________________.

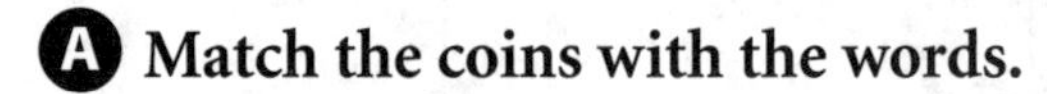

A Match the coins with the words.

a.  b.  c.  d. 

1. nickel c 2. penny ____ 3. quarter ____ 4. dime ____

B Look at the coins in Exercise A. Write the correct amount for each coin.

1. nickel 5¢ 2. penny ______ 3. quarter ______ 4. dime ______

C How much is it? Write the amount.

1. $5.00

2. ________

3. ________

4. ________

D Count the money. Write the total amount.

1. 52¢

2. ________

3. ________

4. ________

E Look at the price tags. Answer the questions.

1. 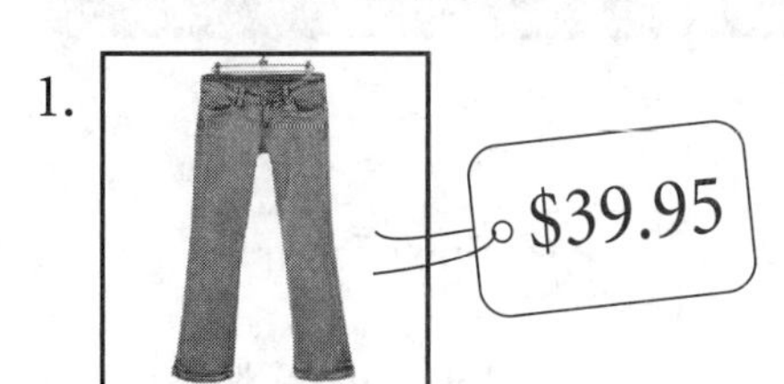

You have $40.00. How much is the change? 5¢

2. $49.99

You have $60.00. How much is the change? ______

3. 

You have $40.00. How much is the change? ______

4. 

You have $65.00. How much is the change? ______

5. 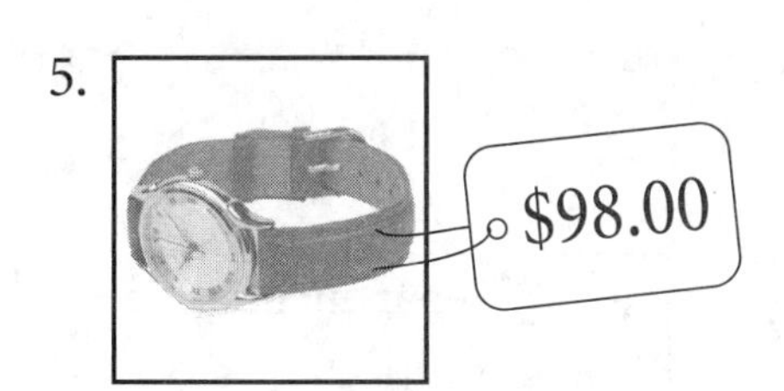

You have $100.00. How much is the change? ______

F Play Track 28. Listen to the conversations. Circle the letter of the correct amount.

1. a. $34.95	(b.) $24.95		4. a. $5.95	b. $9.95
2. a. $37.50	b. $37.60		5. a. $24.50	b. $34.50
3. a. $15.99	b. $14.99		6. a. $49.95	b. $49.99

Read a receipt; Write a personal check

A Look at the receipt for clothes. Answer the questions.

1. What is the name of the store? Joe's Jeans
2. What is the date on the receipt? ____________
3. How much are the jeans? ____________
4. How much are the pants? ____________
5. How much is the T-shirt? ____________
6. How much is the tax? ____________
7. How much are the clothes before tax? ____________
8. How much are the clothes after tax? ____________
9. How much is the change? ____________

Joe's Jeans
587 Fairview Road
Morro Bay, CA 93940
(805) 555-3694

09-15-09

Boys' jeans	29.95
Women's pants	39.95
Boys' T-shirts	12.95
SUBTOTAL	82.85
7% TAX	5.80
TOTAL	88.65
CASH AMOUNT PAID	90.00
CHANGE DUE	1.35

Please keep receipt for returns.
Thank you for shopping at Joe's Jeans.

B Read the receipt. Write a check for the correct amount.

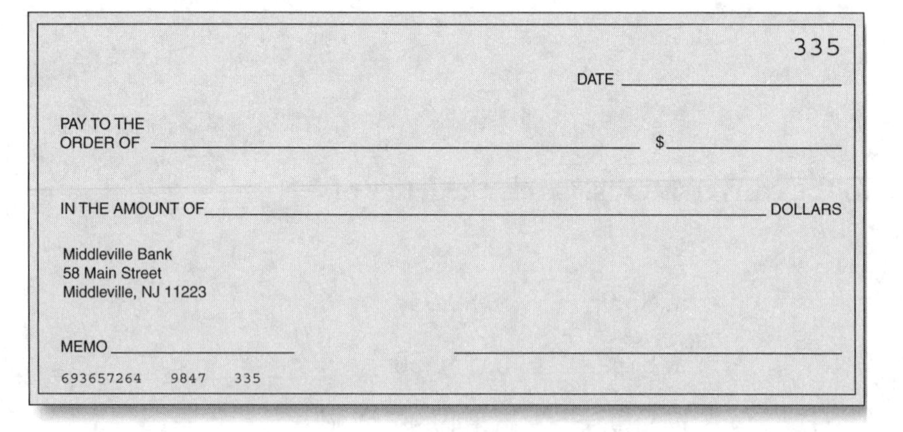
335

DATE ____________

PAY TO THE ORDER OF ____________ $ ____________

IN THE AMOUNT OF ____________ DOLLARS

Middleville Bank
58 Main Street
Middleville, NJ 11223

MEMO ____________ ____________

693657264 9847 335

Ann's Department Store
8 Main St.
Middletown, NY 10941
(845) 555-6790

07-26-09 2:39 P.M.

MEN'S SHIRTS	24.99
WOMEN'S BLOUSES	15.99
WOMEN'S T-SHIRTS	7.99
SUBTOTAL	48.97
TAX 8% ON 48.97	3.92
TOTAL	52.89

A **Complete the conversations with *do* or *does*.**

1. **A:** ___Do___ you have this in blue?
   B: Yes, we ___do___.
2. **A:** __________ Sara like this jacket?
   B: No, she __________.
3. **A:** __________ you need a new jacket?
   B: No, I __________.
4. **A:** __________ Jim need a backpack?
   B: Yes, he __________.
5. **A:** __________ the boys want new sneakers?
   B: Yes, they __________.
6. **A:** __________ Mark and Eric need new jeans?
   B: No, they __________.

B **Unscramble the words to form questions.**

1. Do you have this sweater in a large?
   (have / you / sweater / large / in / do / this / a)
2. ______________________________
   (she / want / does / this / medium / a / T-shirt / in)
3. ______________________________
   (Tom / jacket / have / does / a / black)
4. ______________________________
   (do / like / these / you / shoes)
5. ______________________________
   (blue / you / skirt / have / this / in / do)
6. ______________________________
   (dress / medium / a / do / have / this / you / in)

C **Complete the conversations. Use *do, does, don't,* or *doesn't* and the correct form of the verbs in parentheses.**

1. **A:** ___Do___ you ___have___ this jacket in a small?
   (have)

   B: Yes, we ___do___. Here you go.

2. **A:** __________ he __________ a new wallet?
   (need)

   B: No, he __________. He __________ a wallet.
   (have)

3. **A:** __________ you __________ this watch?
   (like)

   B: Yes, I __________. It's a great watch.

4. **A:** __________ they __________ new shoes for school?
   (need)

   B: No, they __________. They __________ shoes.
   (have)

5. **A:** __________ Monica __________ new sneakers?
   (want)

   B: Yes, she __________. She __________ these sneakers.
   (like)

6. **A:** __________ they __________ this sweater in a large?
   (have)

   B: No, they __________. They __________ a small and a medium.
   (have)

D **Play Track 29. Listen to the conversation. Linda and her mother are at a store. Answer the questions with short answers.**

1. Does Linda need new clothes? ___Yes, she does.___
2. Does she need T-shirts? __________
3. Does she like the green T-shirts? __________
4. Does Linda need pants? __________
5. Does Linda like the blue pants? __________
6. Do they have the pants in a small? __________
7. Does she like the jacket? __________

A Play Track 30. Listen and read.

THE GREENVILLE CITY NEWS

The Greenville City News reporter asks this question:
Do you have nice clothes stores in your country?

Claudia Maldonado

I'm from Quito, Ecuador. In Quito and other big cities in Ecuador, we have many small stores. We have nice clothes stores. If I need a new jacket or new pants, I go to the stores in Quito. But the prices aren't good. In the United States the stores are big. They have a lot of clothes, and the prices are good.

B **Read the article again. Then read the sentences. Circle *True* or *False*.**

1. Quito is in Ecuador. (True) False
2. In Quito all of the stores are big. True False
3. They have nice clothes stores in Quito. True False
4. The prices of the clothes in Quito are good. True False
5. The stores in the United States have a lot of clothes. True False
6. The prices of clothes in the United States are good. True False

C **Are there nice clothes stores in your country? Write true answers. Use Claudia Maldonado's response as a model.**

____

____

____

A **Complete the sentences. Use *don't* or *doesn't*.**

1. They ___don't___ fit.

2. He __________ like it.

3. They __________ match.

4. It __________ fit.

5. They __________ want them.

6. The zipper __________ work.

B **Complete the sentences with *don't* or *doesn't* and the underlined verb.**

1. You <u>need</u> a new sweater. You ___don't need___ a new shirt.
2. I <u>like</u> the blue jacket. I ______________ the black jacket.
3. He <u>likes</u> the blue sneakers. He ______________ the red sneakers.
4. The black shirt <u>fits</u>. The blue shirt ______________.
5. They <u>want</u> new jeans. They ______________ new shoes.
6. She <u>needs</u> a new skirt. She ______________ a new blouse.

C **Rewrite the sentences in the negative. Use contractions.**

1. He likes the red jacket. *He doesn't like the red jacket.*
2. She wants the orange sneakers. ______________________
3. They need new jeans. ______________________
4. I have my receipt. ______________________
5. These pants fit. ______________________
6. This jacket fits. ______________________
7. She has a brown backpack. ______________________

D **Look at the return form. The customer is returning clothes. Write the reasons. Use contractions.**

1. *The shirt doesn't fit.*
2. ______________________
3. ______________________
4. ______________________

Return / Refund Information

Name *Paula Gusto* Phone *(310) 555-9877*

Address *423 Plainview Road*

Santa Monica, CA 90403

Merchandise Returned

Item	Item number	Color	Size	Price	Reason
Shirt	F56006	Blue	S	$29.95	R1
Watch	M32085	Brown		$39.95	R3
Jacket	S42008	Red	M	$69.95	R4
Dress	K3107	White	L	$59.95	R1

Reasons

R1: Doesn't fit **R2:** Doesn't match **R3:** Doesn't work **R4:** Don't like **R5:** Other

Unit 6: Home, Sweet Home

Lesson 1: Vocabulary

A **Which word doesn't belong? Cross it out.**

1. bathtub	toilet	~~sofa~~	shower
2. table	chair	closet	dresser
3. kitchen	sink	bathroom	bedroom
4. microwave	stove	bed	refrigerator
5. dresser	shower	closet	bed

B **Look at the pictures. Complete the sentences.**

1. We need a new microwave .

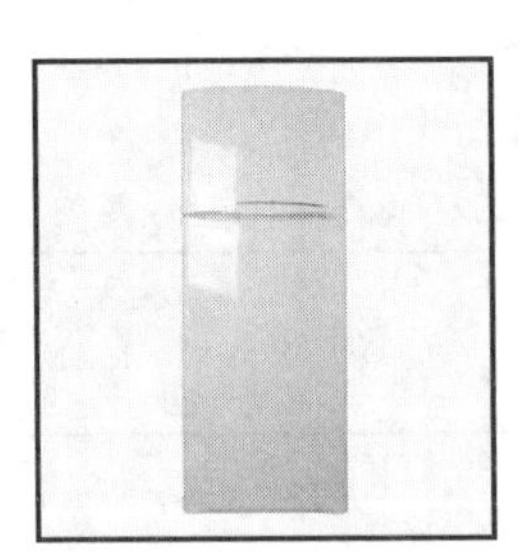

2. Mrs. Sanchez wants a new ______________.

3. Mia needs a new ______________.

4. Mr. Cho wants a new ______________.

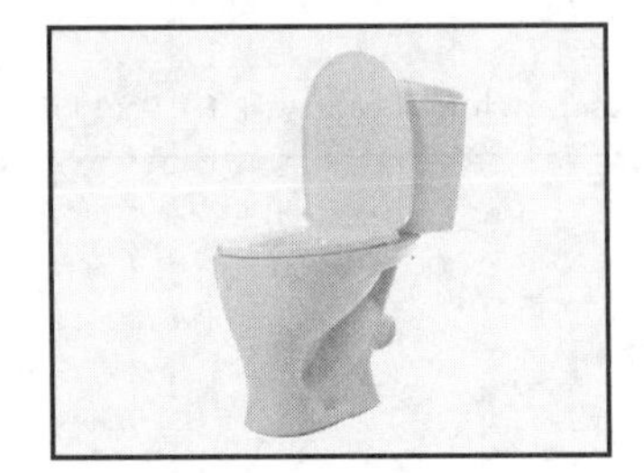

5. Angela needs a new ______________.

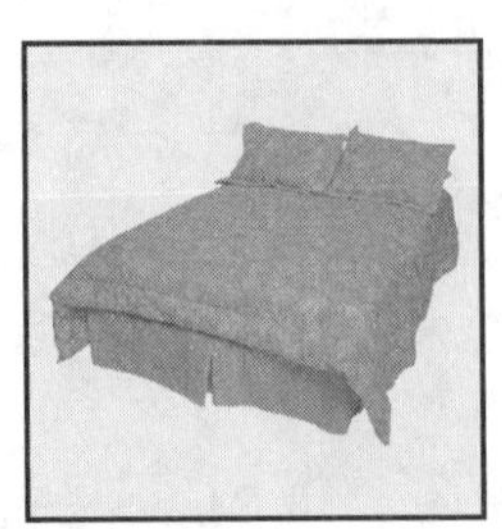

6. I need a new ______________.

C **Look at the pictures. Then look at the floor plan. Give directions. Complete the sentences.**

1.  Please put the ___lamp___ on the table in the ___bedroom___.

2.  Please put the __________ next to the closet in the __________.

3.  Please put the __________ across from the refrigerator in the __________.

4.  Please put the __________ next to the table in the __________.

5.  Please put the __________ next to the sofa in the __________.

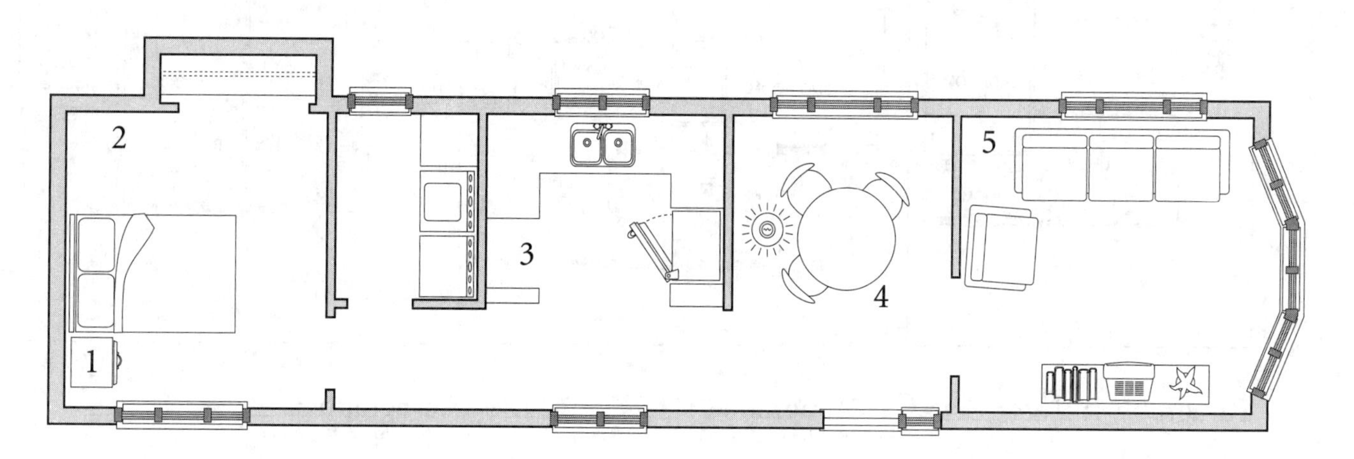

A **Complete the paragraphs. Use *there's* or *there are.***

1. In my house, there's a living room, and there's a small kitchen, but there's no dining room. There are two bedrooms, but ________ no laundry room. ________ one bathroom. ________ a garage. ________ no closets.

2. In my house, ________ a large living room, and ________ a large kitchen, too. ________ a small dining room. ________ two bathrooms and three bedrooms. ________ two closets, also. ________ a laundry room, but ________ no garage.

3. In my house, ________ a living room, but ________ no dining room. ________ one bedroom. ________ one bathroom, but ________ no closets. ________ a kitchen, and ________ a garage.

B **Look at the paragraphs in Exercise A. Match the descriptions with the floor plans.**

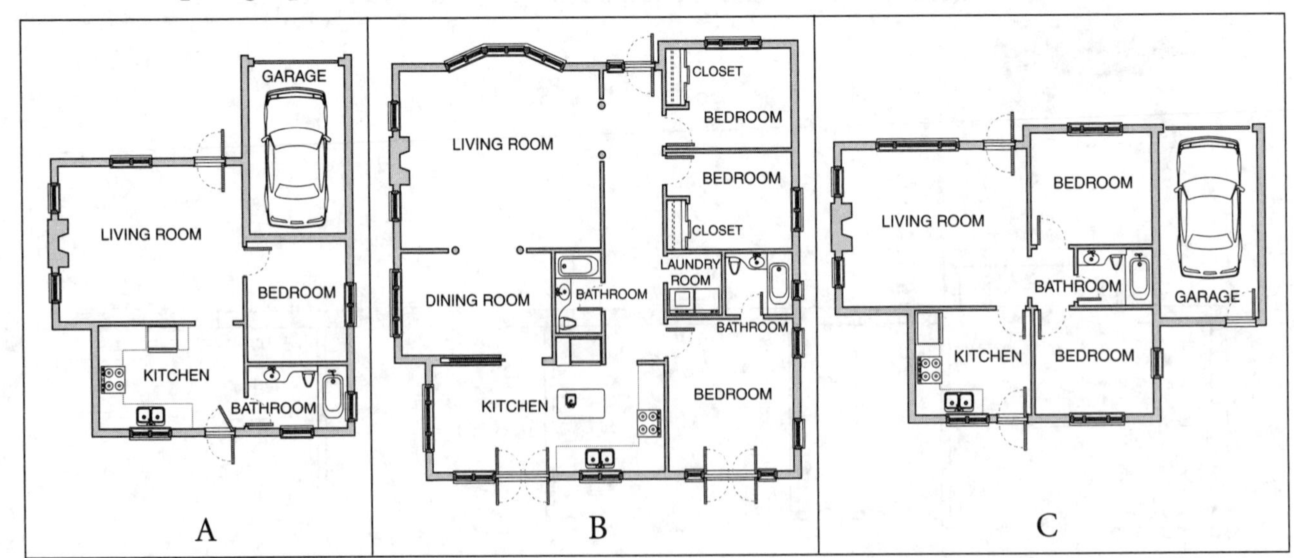

Paragraph 1: Floor Plan C Paragraph 2: ________ Paragraph 3: ________

C Play Track 31. Listen to the sentences. Circle the letter of the correct picture.

1. a. 

   (b.) 

2. a. 

   b. 

3. a. 

   b. 

4. a. 

   b. 

D Look at picture A and read the sentences. Then write sentences about picture B. Use contractions when possible.

chair	lamps	sofa	table

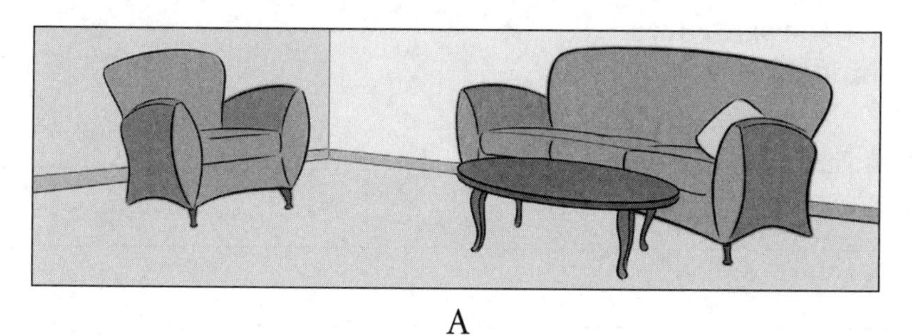

A

B

1. *There's a sofa. There's a table, and there's a chair. There are no lamps.*
2. ______________________________

  **Play Track 32. Listen and read.**

THE GREENVILLE CITY NEWS

The Greenville City News reporter asks this question:
How is your new house?

Sam Robles

My new house is great. We have six rooms in our house. There's a large living room. Next to the living room is a dining room. There's a large sunny kitchen. And we have a small yard. Upstairs there are two bedrooms. One bedroom is very large, and one bedroom is small. And there's one bathroom. There are five closets in the house. And there's a garage. We're very happy in our new house!

B Read the article again. Then complete the sentences. Underline the correct words.

1. There's a **large** / **small** living room.
2. The dining room is next to the **kitchen** / **living room**.
3. The **dining room** / **kitchen** is sunny.
4. There's a **small** / **large** yard.
5. There are **two** / **three** bedrooms.
6. There are **three** / **five** closets in the house.
7. There's a **laundry room** / **garage**.

C Write about your home. Complete the sentences.
Use Sam Robles's response as a model.

There are ___________ rooms in my home. There's ______________________________

____

____

A **Look at the picture. Ask and answer the questions. Use contractions when possible.**

1. ___Is there___ a sofa? ___Yes, there is.___
2. ____________ a dining room? ____________
3. ____________ a kitchen table? ____________
4. ____________ a refrigerator? ____________
5. ____________ chairs? ____________
6. ____________ floor lamps? ____________
7. ____________ a laundry room? ____________
8. ____________ a microwave? ____________
9. ____________ a stove? ____________
10. ____________ closets? ____________

B **Look at the apartment ads. Complete the conversations. Use the words in parentheses. Use contractions when possible.**

1. A: (studio apartment) Is there a studio apartment for rent?
   B: Yes, there is. There's an unfurnished apartment for rent.
   A: (refrigerator) ____________________
   B: Yes, there is. There's a new refrigerator.
   A: (closets) ____________________
   B: ____________________
   A: (stove) ____________________
   B: No, there's no stove.

> **FOR RENT**
> **Studio Apartment**
> Unfurnished,
> new refrigerator,
> large bathroom,
> very sunny

2. A: (one-bedroom apartment) ____________________
   B: ____________________
   A: (appliances) ____________________
   B: ____________________
   A: (bed) ____________________
   B: ____________________
   A: (dining room) ____________________
   B: ____________________

> **FOR RENT**
> **1-Bedroom Furnished Apartment:** large new kitchen, new appliances, 3 closets, new bed, sofa and table

3. A: (two-bedroom apartment) ____________________
   B: ____________________
   A: (microwave) ____________________
   B: ____________________
   A: (closets) ____________________
   B: ____________________
   A: (laundry room) ____________________
   B: ____________________

> **FOR RENT**
> **2-Bedroom Unfurnished Apartment:** new bathroom, microwave, 4 closets, large living room

Lesson 7: Read addresses and apartment ads

A **Play Track 33. Listen. Circle the letter of the correct address.**

1. a. 365 Meadow Street | (b.) 365 Meadow Drive | c. 365 Meadow Avenue
2. a. 52 Park Boulevard | b. 52 Park Street | c. 52 Park Road
3. a. 45 Orange Lane | b. 45 Orange Avenue | c. 45 Orange Road
4. a. 37 Sutton Street | b. 37 Sutton Avenue | c. 37 Sutton Boulevard
5. a. 145 Drake Road | b. 145 Drake Street | c. 145 Drake Avenue

B **Write the abbreviations.**

1. Street ___St.___
2. Drive ________
3. Avenue ________
4. Boulevard ________
5. Road ________

C **Look at the ad. Write three descriptions. Do not use abbreviations.**

FOR RENT

2-BR Apt: Lg Kit, DR,
A/C, Pkg, Utils. incl.
$1,800 month

There's a two-bedroom apartment for rent.

____

____

____

D **Match the parts of the conversations.**

1. What's the address? c
2. How much is the apartment? ____
3. Does it have parking? ____
4. Does it have a new kitchen? ____
5. Is there a laundry room? ____

a. Yes, it does.
b. No, but the stove is new.
c. It's 3205 Baker Place.
d. Yes, there is.
e. It's $1,200 a month.

E **Play Track 34. Listen to the conversations. Complete the ads. Use abbreviations.**

1.

FOR RENT

1 BR/1 BA Apt.

$1200 a month

Lg ________ with new stove

____

14 Bank St., Apt. 3D

(406) 555-1890

2.

FOR RENT

2 BR/1 BA Apt.

$1300 a month

Lg ________ with new shower

________ ________

346 Clover Blvd., Apt. 1C

(317) 555-1299

3.

FOR RENT

3 BR/2 BA Apt. in new ________

$1450 a month

Lg ________

45 Orchard ________, Apt. 2B

(836) 555-6978

4.

FOR RENT

1 BR/1 BA Apt.

$900 a month

Lg ________

________ room in bldg.

3 Apple ________, Apt. 2A

(479) 555-6709

Address an envelope

A You need to send a check for your rent to Mr. David Anders. His address is 456 Oppenheimer Street, Lacie, New Jersey, 08021. Address the envelope. Write your return address.

B Address the envelope to someone you know.

A **Complete the sentences. Use *from, to, in, at,* or *on.***

1. Carmen is coming ___from___ home.
2. It's ______ 554 Benson Avenue.
3. The hotel is ______ Greenville.
4. I'm going ______ the store.
5. My office is ______ Main Street.
6. Turn right ______ the third light.

B **Complete the conversation. Use *from, on,* or *at.***

A: How do I get to Century Department Store?

B: ___From___ here? Let's see. Go east ______ Maple Avenue. Turn left ______ Bank Street. Then continue ______ Bank Street to 6th Street. It's ______ the corner of Bank and 6th.

C **Complete the conversation. Use *from, to, in, at,* or *on.***

Sam: Hi, Jess. Are you coming ___to___ my house?

Jess: Yes, Sam. How do I get there ______ here? I'm coming ______ my office.

Sam: My apartment is ______ Oakdale. First, go ______ Conner Street. Turn left. Continue north ______ Conner Street. Then turn left ______ the light. That's Manor Road. My house is ______ 58 Manor Road.

Jess: Great!

D Play Track 35. Listen to the directions. Complete the directions. Underline the correct words.

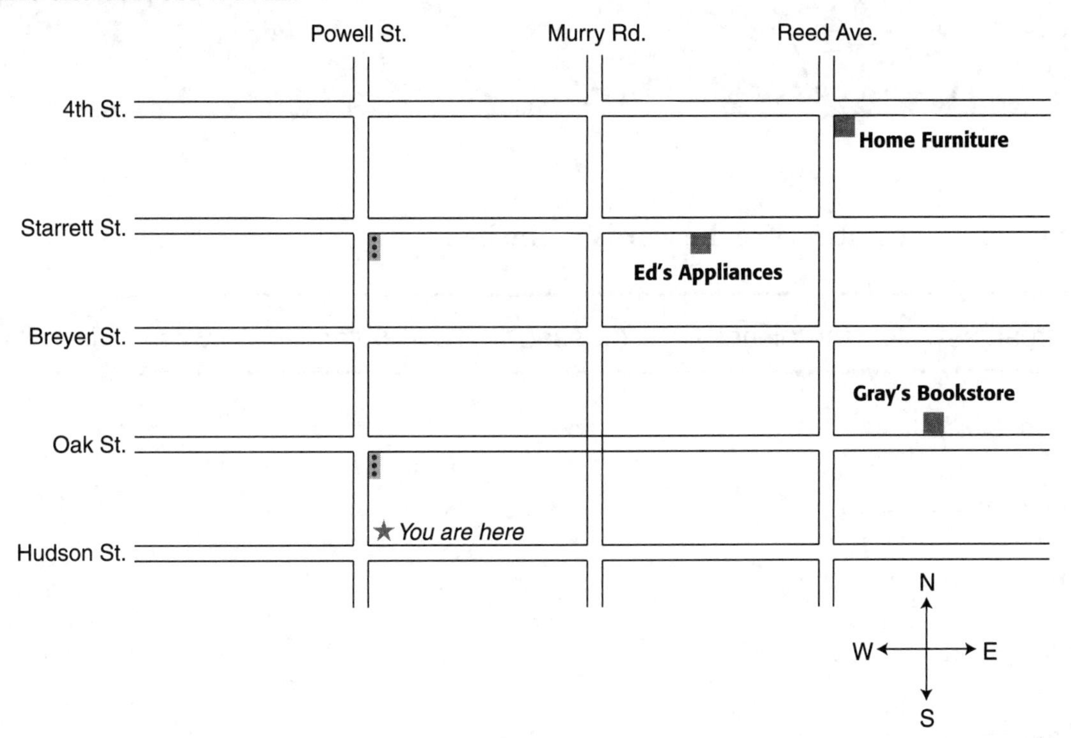

Go (**south** / **north**) (**in** / **on**) Powell Street. Continue (**at** / **on**) Powell Street for three blocks. Turn right (**on** / **at**) the (**3rd** / **2nd**) light. Continue (**east** / **west**) (**in** / **on**) Starrett Street. Our store is (**at** / **on**) Starrett Street (**in** / **on**) the (**left** / **right**). It's (**at** / **in**) 3228 Starrett Street.

E **Look at the map. You are at the corner of Powell and Hudson. Read the directions in Exercise D. Where are you?**

I'm at ______________________.

F **Look at the map in Exercise D. You are at the corner of 4th and Powell. Complete the directions to Gray's Bookstore.**

Go ___south___ __________ Powell Street. Continue __________ Powell Street for one block. Turn left __________ the light. Continue __________ Starrett Street for two blocks. Go __________ on Reed Avenue. Continue __________ Reed Avenue for two blocks. Turn __________ on Oak Street. It's __________ 4118 Oak Street.

Unit 7: Day After Day

Lesson 1: Vocabulary

A **Complete the activities. Use the words in the box.**

breakfast	~~the dishes~~	dressed	a shower	to work

1. wash _the dishes_
2. eat ______
3. go ______
4. take ______
5. get ______

B **Look at Tanya's schedule for the evening. Complete the sentences.**

1. She _gets home_ at 5:30.
2. She ______ from 6:00 to 7:00.
3. She ______ at 7:00.
4. At 7:30 she ______.
5. At 8:00 she ______ and ______.
6. From 8:30 to 9:30 she ______.
7. She ______ at 9:30.
8. At 10:00 she ______.

5:30 P.M. get home
6:00 – 7:00 exercise
7:00 cook dinner
7:30 eat dinner
8:00 wash the dishes/watch TV
8:30 – 9:30 read the newspaper
9:30 take a shower
10:00 go to sleep

C **Look at the pictures. Complete the conversations.**

1. **A:** What time does Max ___get up___?

   B: At ___5:00___.

2. **A:** What time does he ________________?

   B: At ________________.

3. **A:** What time does he ________________?

   B: At ________________.

4. **A:** What time does he ________________?

   B: At ________________.

5. **A:** What time does he ________________?

   B: At ________________.

D **Write about yourself. What is your schedule like? Complete the sentences.**

I get up at ________________.

I eat breakfast at ________________.

I go to **work** / **school** at ________________.

A **Complete the conversations. Use the verbs in parentheses. Use the simple present.**

1. (work) A: When ___do___ you ___work___? B: On Saturdays.
2. (get up) A: What time ___does___ she ___get up___? B: At 7:00.
3. (have) A: When __________ they __________ class? B: From 6:00 to 8:00.
4. (go) A: What time __________ you __________ to work? B: At 9:00.
5. (start) A: When __________ the movie __________? B: At 7:45.
6. (get) A: What time __________ she __________ home? B: At 5:30.

B **Make questions with *what time*. Use the words in parentheses. Then look at the clocks. Answer the questions.**

1. (you / get home)
   A: What time do you get home?
   B: At 6:30.
2. (they / go to work)
   A: ____________________
   B: ____________________
3. (Arnold / exercise)
   A: ____________________
   B: ____________________
4. (she / eat breakfast)
   A: ____________________
   B: ____________________
5. (Jason and Marie / eat dinner)
   A: ____________________
   B: ____________________

C Complete the conversations. Use *on, at, from,* or *to.*

1. **A:** When does Maria play soccer?

   B: From 10:00 to 12:00 on Saturdays.

2. **A:** When does Jack take a computer class?

   B: ________ Tuesdays.

3. **A:** When does Paul watch TV?

   B: ________ 8:00 ________ 10:00.

4. **A:** When does your English class start?

   B: ________ 7:00.

5. **A:** When do they get up?

   B: ________ 10:00 ________ Saturdays.

D Look at Samantha's schedule. Complete the conversations.

Sunday	Monday	Tuesday	Wednesday	Thursday	Friday	Saturday
12:00–5:00 work	4:00–6:00 study with Martha	7:00–9:00 English class	7:00–9:00 English class	4:00–7:00 soccer	3:00–6:00 babysit	9:30–11:30 soccer 1:00–3:00 computer class

1. **A:** Is Samantha free on Sundays at 4:00?

   B: No. She works on Sundays from 12:00–5:00.

2. **A:** Is she free on Wednesdays at 8:00?

   B: No. ________________________________

3. **A:** Is she free on Thursdays at 6:00?

   B: No. ________________________________

4. **A:** Is she free on Fridays at 5:00?

   B: No. ________________________________

5. **A:** Is she free on Saturdays at 2:00?

   B: No. ________________________________

A Play Track 36. Listen to the conversation. Complete the schedule. Write the times and the activities.

Sunday	Monday	Tuesday	Wednesday	Thursday	Friday	Saturday
		10:00–2:00 work				

B Look at the time sheet. Complete the sentences.

TIME SHEET			
EMPLOYEE NAME Last First Roberts, Clara		EMPLOYEE I.D. # 5470998	
		Week ending 10/15	
DAY	TIME IN	TIME OUT	HOURS
Mon.	off		
Tues.	7:00 P.M.	12:00 A.M.	5
Wed.	off		
Thurs.	7:00 P.M.	12:00 A.M.	5
Fri.	off		
Sat.	9:00 A.M.	1:00 P.M.	4
Sun.	6:00 A.M.	12:00 P.M.	6
Employee Signature Clara Roberts		TOTAL HOURS 20	

1. Clara works from 7:00 P.M. to 12:00 A.M. on Tuesdays and Thursdays.
2. She is off on ______, ______, and ______.
3. She starts work at ______ on Saturdays.
4. She finishes work at ______ on Saturdays.
5. She works from ______ to ______ on Sundays.
6. She works ______ hours a week.

C **Look at the time sheet. Complete the conversations.**

TIME SHEET			
EMPLOYEE NAME Last First Chu, Martin		EMPLOYEE I.D. # 459-34-9876	
			Week ending 7/15
DAY	TIME IN	TIME OUT	HOURS
Mon.	off		
Tues.	11:00 A.M.	7:00 P.M.	8
Wed.	off		
Thurs.	11:00 A.M.	7:00 P.M.	8
Fri.	off		
Sat.	8:00 A.M.	2:00 P.M.	6
Sun.	off		
Employee Signature Martin Chu		TOTAL HOURS 22	

1. **A:** When does Martin work?

   B: He works on Tuesdays, ___________, and ___________.

2. **A:** What time does he start work on Tuesdays?

   B: At ___________.

3. **A:** When does he work on Thursdays?

   B: He works from ___________ to ___________.

4. **A:** What time does he start work on Saturdays?

   B: At ___________.

5. **A:** When does he finish work at 2:00?

   B: On ___________.

D **What about you? Complete the sentences.**

I **work / go to school** ___________ **days / hours** a week. I **work / go to school** on ___________ from ___________ to ___________.

Complete a time sheet; Write a note about vacation time

A **Read the information. Complete the time sheet for Elisa Vlahos for the week ending November 14. Her employee ID number is 459876.**

TIME SHEET			
EMPLOYEE NAME **Last** Vlahos **First**		**EMPLOYEE I.D. #**	
		Week ending	
DAY	**TIME IN**	**TIME OUT**	**HOURS**
Mon.			
Tues.			
Wed.			
Thurs.			
Fri.			
Sat.			
Sun.			
Employee Signature Elisa Vlahos		**TOTAL HOURS**	

My name is Elisa Vlahos. I'm a nurse at Waterside Community Hospital. I work Sunday to Thursday. My hours are 4:00 to 11:00 P.M.

B **You need to take a vacation day next Friday, May 12. Write a note to your manager. Ask for permission to take the day off.**

A Look at the calendar. Complete the sentences. Use *always, usually, sometimes,* or *never.*

February

Sunday	Monday	Tuesday	Wednesday	Thursday	Friday	Saturday
1 beach	2 Work 10:00 – 2:00	3 Work 10:00 – 2:00	4 Work 10:00 – 2:00	5 Work 10:00 – 2:00	6 Work 10:00 – 2:00 do laundry play basketball	7
8 beach	9 Work 10:00 – 2:00	10 Work 10:00 – 2:00	11 Work 10:00 – 2:00	12 Work 10:00 – 2:00	13 Work 10:00 – 2:00 do laundry play basketball	14 go dancing
15 beach	16 Work 10:00 – 2:00	17 Work 10:00 – 2:00	18 Work 10:00 – 2:00	19 Work 10:00 – 2:00	20 Work 10:00 – 2:00 do laundry play basketball	21
22 beach	23 Work 10:00 – 2:00	24 Work 10:00 – 2:00	25 Work 10:00 – 2:00	26 Work 10:00 – 2:00	27 Work 10:00 – 2:00 do laundry	28

1. Huong ___always___ goes to the beach on Sundays.
2. She __________ works from 10:00 A.M. to 2:00 P.M. Mondays to Fridays.
3. She __________ does laundry on Fridays.
4. She __________ plays basketball on Friday nights.
5. She __________ goes dancing on Saturday nights.
6. She __________ plays basketball on Saturday nights.

B Unscramble the words to form sentences.

1. ___Sarah usually shops for food on Saturdays.___
(Sarah / Saturdays / shops for food / usually / on)
2. ____________________
(Martin / takes a shower / always / at night)
3. ____________________
(Conor / on / rides his bike / Sundays / sometimes)
4. ____________________
(they / on / never / do the laundry / Sundays)

C Look at the pictures. Complete the conversations.

1. **A:** What does Paco usually do on Saturdays?

   B: He usually goes to the park.

2. **A:** What does Elena sometimes do on Sundays?

   B: ____________________

3. **A:** What does Mr. Garcia always do on Saturdays?

   B: ____________________

4. **A:** What does Mr. Kim never do on Saturday nights?

   B: ____________________

5. **A:** What does Mei-Li sometimes do on Sundays?

   B: ____________________

6. **A:** What does Teresa always do on Sundays?

   B: ____________________

D Complete the sentences. Write about your weekend activities.

1. I always ____________________.
2. I usually ____________________.
3. I sometimes ____________________.
4. I never ____________________.

A  **Play Track 37. Listen and read.**

THE GREENVILLE CITY NEWS

The Greenville City News reporter asks this question:
How much free time do you have?

Irma Garza

I don't have much free time. I have a busy schedule. I have a husband and two small children. I work on Mondays, Wednesdays, and Thursdays from 6:00 to 11:00 P.M. I work at night because my husband works days. I don't need a babysitter at night. My husband works on Saturdays, too. I shop for food and clean the house on Saturdays. On Sundays, we take the children to the park or the zoo. I don't really have any free time.

B Read the article again. The sentences below have mistakes. Correct the mistakes.

1. Irma works ~~in the mornings~~ at night.
2. She works two nights a week.
3. Her husband works at night.
4. She works on Saturdays.
5. Her husband shops for food.
6. On Saturdays, Irma and her husband take the children to the park or zoo.

C Complete the sentences. What do you do on weekends?

On Saturdays, I usually ____________________.

On Sundays, I ____________________.

A **Look at Brad's schedule. Complete the conversations.**

October 5–11						
SUN	MON	TUES	WED	THURS	FRI	SAT
go running 7:00–8:00 study English 10:00–12:00 work on car 2:00–3:00 play basketball 4:00–5:00	go running 7:00–8:00 work 10:00–3:00 class 7:00–9:30	go running 7:00–8:00 work 10:00–3:00 class 7:00–9:30	go running 7:00–8:00 work 10:00–3:00 class 7:00–9:30	go running 7:00–8:00 work 10:00–3:00 class 7:00–9:30	go running 7:00–8:00 work 10:00–3:00 shop for food 4:00	go running 7:00–8:00 study English 9:00–11:00 work on car 2:00–3:00 see a movie 7:00

1. **A:** How often does Brad go running?
   B: He goes running every day.
2. **A:** How often does he study English?
   B: ______________________________
3. **A:** How often does he work on his car?
   B: ______________________________
4. **A:** How often does he play basketball?
   B: ______________________________
5. **A:** How often does he work?
   B: ______________________________
6. **A:** How often does he have class?
   B: ______________________________
7. **A:** How often does he shop for food?
   B: ______________________________
8. **A:** How often does he see a movie?
   B: ______________________________

B Play Track 38. Listen to the conversation. Check (✓) the correct columns in the chart.

	Once a week	Three times a week	Every day	Never
Go running		✓		
Take a long walk				
Do puzzles				
Listen to music				

C Complete the questions. Use the verbs in parentheses. Use the simple present.

1. (listen to music) How often ___does___ José ___listen to music___?
2. (go running) How often ________ you ________________?
3. (play video games) How often ________ Sam and Mark ________________?
4. (ride her bike) How often ________ your mother ________________?
5. (work) How often ________ Yolanda ________________?
6. (have English class) How often ________ your friends ________________?

D Complete the sentences about yourself. Use the ideas in the box.

when I go to a party	when I go to school	when I listen to music
when I see my friends	when I take a test	when I watch a sad movie

1. I feel relaxed ________________________________.
2. I feel bored ________________________________.
3. I feel stressed ________________________________.
4. I feel sad ________________________________.
5. I feel happy ________________________________.
6. I feel excited ________________________________.

Unit 8: From Soup to Nuts

Lesson 1: Vocabulary

A What's for breakfast? Match the words with the pictures.

apples	bananas	bread	butter
cereal	eggs	oranges	~~yogurt~~

1. yogurt
2. ______
3. ______
4. ______
5. ______
6. ______
7. ______
8. ______

B Look at the pictures. Write the names of the foods.

1. cabbage
2. ______
3. ______
4. ______
5. ______

6. ______
7. ______
8. ______
9. ______
10. ______

C **Look at the chart. How often does Ada eat each kind of food? Complete the sentences.**

	Never	Once a day	Twice a day	3–5 times a day
Grains		x		
Vegetables			x	
Fruit	x			
Meat and beans				x
Dairy		x		

1. Ada eats ___grains___ once a day.
2. She eats __________ twice a day.
3. She never eats __________.
4. She eats __________ and __________ three to five times a day.
5. She has __________ once a day.

D **How often do you eat these foods? Complete the chart with your own information.**

	Never	Once a day	Twice a day	3–5 times a day
Grains				
Vegetables				
Fruit				
Meat and beans				
Dairy				

E **Look at the chart in Exercise D. Write sentences. Use the sentence below as a model.**

I eat grains three times a day.

1. ______________________________
2. ______________________________
3. ______________________________
4. ______________________________
5. ______________________________

A **Complete the chart. Put the foods in the correct column.**

~~apple~~	~~beef~~	butter	cake	cereal	cookie
egg	lettuce	pancake	potato	taco	yogurt

Count			Non-count		
apple	______	______	beef	______	______
______	______	______	______	______	______

B **Look at the pictures. Complete the sentences. Write the correct food and *it* or *them*.**

1. I like bananas.
   I eat them every day.

2. I love steak.
   I eat it with onions.

3. I love ______.
   I eat ______ for lunch every day.

4. I usually have ______ for breakfast.
   I eat ______ before I go to work.

5. I eat ______ once a day.
   I have ______ with dinner.

6. I usually have ______ for breakfast.
   I eat ______ with cheese.

C Look at the pictures. Complete the conversations.

1. **A:** Do you like eggs?

   B: Not really. I like _pancakes_.

2. **A:** Do you want an apple?

   B: No, thanks.

   I don't really like ____________.

3. **A:** Do you like bananas?

   B: Not really. I like ____________.

4. **A:** Do you want a vegetable for dinner?

   B: Yes, I'd like ____________.

5. **A:** Do you want apple pie for dessert?

   B: No, thanks. I don't really like ____________.

6. **A:** What do you want for lunch?

   B: I want ____________.

D Complete the conversation. Use the words in parentheses in the singular or plural. Add *a* when necessary.

1. **A:** Wow, I'm really hungry.

   B: Me, too. What do you want?

   A: First I want (hamburger) _a hamburger_.

   B: First?

2. **A:** Yeah, then I want (taco) _a taco_. I love _tacos_.

   B: I want ____________, too.

3. **A:** Then I want (pizza) ____________.

   B: ____________? What kind of ____________ do you want?

   A: Cheese. I want cheese ____________. And I want a large iced tea.

4. **B:** And dessert?

   A: Oh, yes! I want (cake) ____________. Do they have ____________?

Write a shopping list; Write a note about what you need

A **Read the conversation. Then complete the shopping list.**

A: We need a lot of food.

B: I know. There's no milk.

A: Right. We need milk and orange juice.

B: OK. What about vegetables?

A: We need four tomatoes and three onions.

B: What about meat for dinner?

A: Yes, get steak.

B: Do we need cheese?

A: Yes, get cheese, also.

B: OK. Anything else?

A: Yes, we need bread and cereal. And we need pasta, too.

B: OK.

A: I think that's everything.

Shopping List

milk
____
____
4 __________
____
____
____
____
cereal
____

B **Write a note about things you need at the store. Use true or made-up information.**

A **Play Track 39. Listen and read.**

THE GREENVILLE CITY NEWS

The Greenville City News reporter asks these questions:
Do you eat healthy foods? How often do you eat them?

Keisha Clarke

I usually eat healthy foods. I have cereal and fruit for breakfast every day. I sometimes have a hamburger for lunch, but usually I have a salad. For dinner, I usually have chicken and potatoes. And I always have a green vegetable, like green beans. I love vegetables.

Derek Jablonski

I don't always eat right. I never eat breakfast because I don't have time. I only have a half-hour for lunch, so I usually eat a hamburger and a piece of cake. For dinner, I eat pizza a lot—four or five times a week. I love pizza!

B **Read the article again. Then read the sentences. Circle *True* or *False*.**

1. Keisha eats breakfast every day.	(True)	False
2. Derek eats cereal every day.	True	False
3. Keisha eats chicken and potatoes for lunch.	True	False
4. Derek eats hamburgers for lunch.	True	False
5. Keisha eats green vegetables every day.	True	False
6. Derek doesn't often eat pizza.	True	False

C **What do you think? Who eats healthy foods? Complete the sentences.**

I think **Derek / Keisha** eats healthy foods. __________ eats __________ and __________.
These are healthy foods.

A **Make *or* questions with *want.* Use the words in parentheses.**

1. (iced tea / coffee) Do you want iced tea or coffee?
2. (fries / salad) ______
3. (pizza / a sandwich) ______
4. (fries / a baked potato) ______
5. (milk / juice) ______
6. (steak / a hamburger) ______

B **Look at the pictures. Make *or* questions with *would like.***

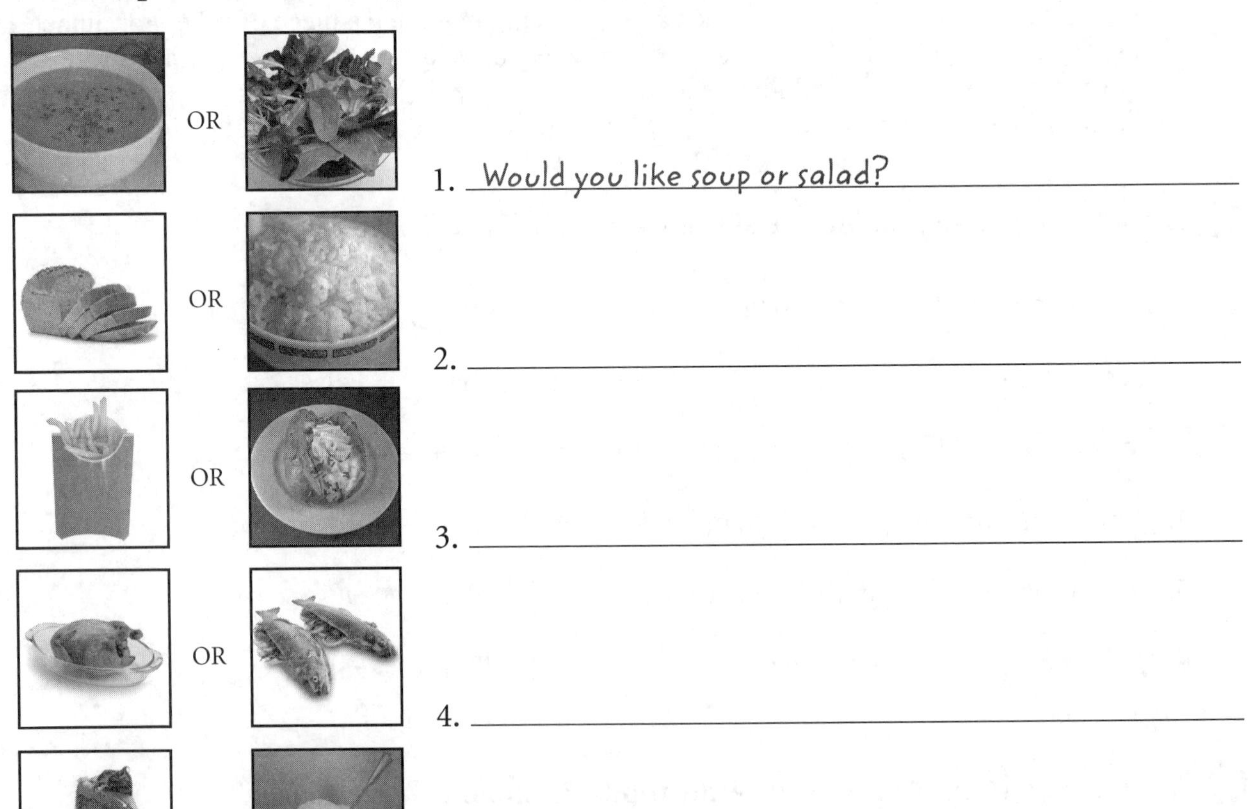

OR

1. Would you like soup or salad?
2. ______
3. ______
4. ______
5. ______

C **Match the questions with the responses. Circle the letter of the correct answer.**

1. Do you like vegetables?

   (a.) Yes. I really like cabbage. b. Yes, I'd really like cabbage.

2. Can I help you?

   a. I like pizza. b. Yes. I'd like a pizza.

3. Anything to drink?

   a. I like water. b. I'd like water, please.

4. Do you want a baked potato or fries?

   a. I like baked potatoes. b. I'd like a baked potato.

5. Would you like juice or soda?

   a. I like juice. b. I'd like juice.

6. Do you like steak?

   a. Not really. I like chicken. b. Not really. I'd like chicken.

D **Play Track 40. Listen to the conversation. Write the order.**

Date				

Burger Heaven
Guest Check

	a green salad	

A **Look at the pictures. Form questions with *How much / How many.* Answer the questions with *A lot* or *Not many / Not much.***

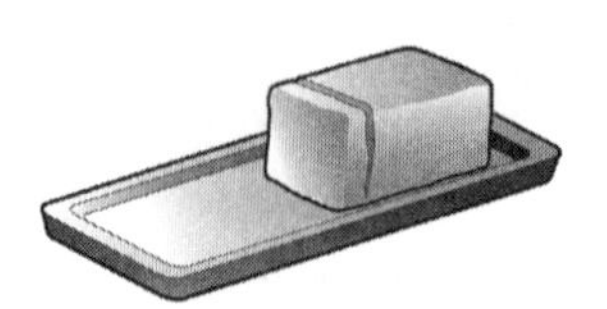

1. A: How much butter is there?
   B: Not much. We need to buy more.

2. A: How many onions do we have?
   B: Not many. We only have two. Let's get some more.

3. A: ____________________ is there?
   B: ____________________. We don't need to get more.

4. A: ____________________ is there?
   B: ____________________. We need to get more.

5. A: ____________________ is there?
   B: ____________________. We don't need to get more.

6. A: ____________________ do we have?
   B: ____________________. We have three large boxes!

7. A: ____________________ are there?
   B: ____________________. We only have two.

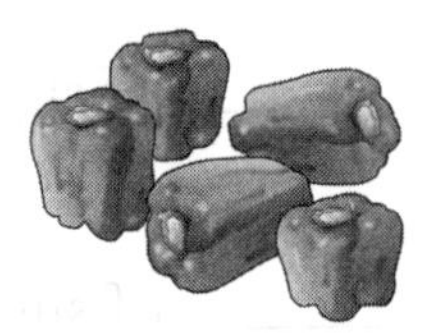

8. A: ____________________ do we have?
   B: ____________________. And they're big!

B Look at the recipe. Ask questions. Use *much* or *many* and the words in parentheses. Then write answers.

1. **A:** How ___much turkey___ do we need?
   (**turkey**)
   B: We need ___two pounds___.
2. **A:** How ____________________?
   (**rice**)
   B: We need ____________________.
3. **A:** How ____________________?
   (**peppers**)
   B: We need ____________________.
4. **A:** How ____________________?
   (**onions**)
   B: We need ____________________.
5. **A:** How ____________________?
   (**milk**)
   B: We need ____________________.
6. **A:** How ____________________?
   (**cheese**)
   B: We need ____________________.
7. **A:** How ____________________?
   (**vegetable oil**)
   B: We need ____________________.

Turkey and rice casserole

Ingredients:

2 lbs. turkey
12 oz. rice
2 small peppers
3 small onions
8 oz. milk
10 oz. cheese
2 oz. vegetable oil

C Play Track 42. Listen to the conversation. Paul and Marie are planning a party. Which foods are they having? Check (✓) the foods.

- ☑ apple pie
- ☐ cake
- ☐ fried chicken
- ☐ fries
- ☐ green salad
- ☐ grilled chicken
- ☐ juice
- ☐ rice
- ☐ soda
- ☐ soup
- ☐ tea
- ☐ water

Unit 9: Rain or Shine

Lesson 1: Vocabulary

A **Look at the thermometer. Label it with the words *cold, warm, hot,* and *cool.***

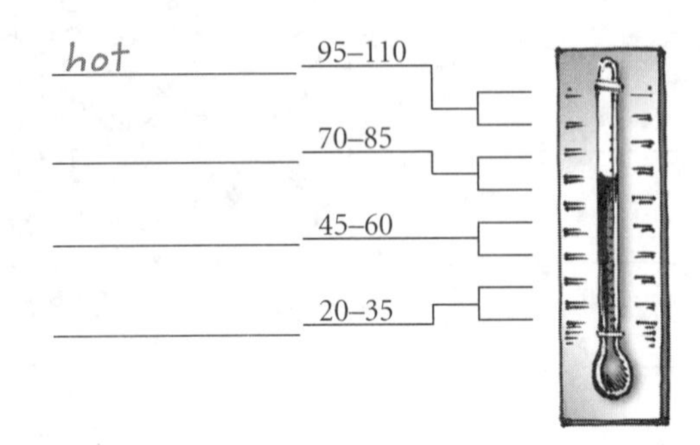

B **Match the seasons with the pictures.**

a.

b.

c.

d.

1. winter __c__ 2. spring ____ 3. summer ____ 4. fall ____

C **Look at the pictures. Write sentences about each scene. Use the words in the box.**

~~cloudy~~	cold	cool	hot	rainy	snowy	sunny	~~warm~~

1. It's warm and cloudy.

2. ______________________________

3. ______________________________

4. ______________________________

D **What seasons does your country have? What is the weather like? Write sentences.**

In my country, ______________________________

____

____

____

A **Complete the sentences. Use the verbs in parentheses.**

1. Kara ___is not working___ in her office today. She's at home.
   (not work)
2. Carl and Martha ______________________ their daughter at college.
   (visit)
3. Bruno ______________________ on the sofa. He's in the bedroom now.
   (not sleep)
4. Stephanie ______________________ in the library.
   (study)
5. Roman and Cara ______________________ lunch today. They're in a meeting now.
   (not eat)
6. Kira and Rob ______________________ dinner for us.
   (make)

B **Unscramble the words to form sentences. Use contractions.**

1. ___She's talking on the phone.___
   (she / phone / talking / on / is / the)
2. ______________________
   (are / we / TV / watching)
3. ______________________
   (am / reading / a / I / book)
4. ______________________
   (raining / is / Chicago / it / in)
5. ______________________
   (is / he / his / riding / bike)
6. ______________________
   (they / the / running / park / in / are)
7. ______________________
   (is / she / wearing / jacket / new / a)
8. ______________________
   (visiting / we / in / are / friends / Miami / our)

C **Look at the picture. Complete the sentences with *'s, isn't, 're,* or *aren't,* and the verbs in parentheses.**

1. She _'s talking_ __________ on the phone. (**talk**)
2. She ____________________ water. (**drink**)
3. She ____________________. (**eat**)
4. She ____________________ her homework. (**do**)
5. He ____________________ to music. (**listen**)
6. He ____________________ his homework. (**do**)
7. He ____________________ water. (**drink**)
8. He ____________________ on the phone. (**talk**)

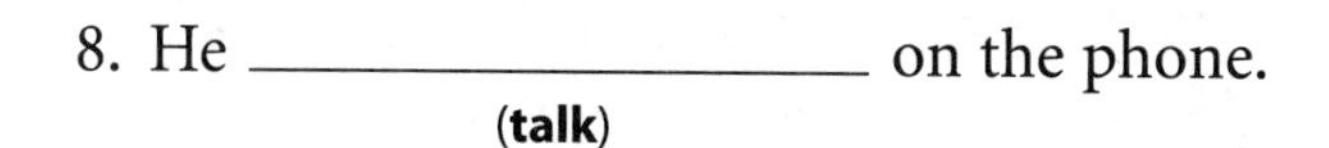

9. They ____________________ in the kitchen. (**sit**)
10. They ____________________. (**watch TV**)

D **Look at the picture. Describe what you see. Use the verbs in the box.**

~~clean~~	cook	listen to music	read	sleep

1. _He's cleaning._ ____________________
2. ____________________
3. ____________________
4. ____________________
5. ____________________

Write a postcard

Look at the picture and the information. Then write a postcard from Joanna to her friend.

Joanna is on vacation. She's in Los Angeles. She's visiting her cousin Ramon. He's at work now.

Hi Jamie,

See you soon!

Joanna

Joanna Ramirez
15 Jessup Court
Los Angeles, CA 90053

Jamie Smith
3 Park Place
Middletown, NY 10940

A **Match the advice with the emergencies.**

a. an earthquake

b. a tornado

c. a heat wave

d. a flood

e. a thunderstorm

f. a hurricane

1. Stay in the house. __d__
2. Go downstairs. ____
3. Cover your windows. ____
4. Don't go swimming. ____
5. Drink a lot of water. ____
6. Go under a piece of furniture, like a desk. ____

B **Play Track 43. Listen to the conversation. Circle the items you hear.**

C **Write sentences about what to do in bad weather. Use the example below as a model.**

Buy batteries and candles.

1. A thunderstorm

____

2. A snowstorm

____

3. A wild fire

____

D **Which type of bad weather do you have in your country?**

In my country, ______________________________

____

____

E **Fill out the emergency plan for your family.**

Emergency Family Plan
Places to meet
1. 2.
Emergency phone numbers

A **Look at the pictures. Answer the questions with short answers. Use contractions when possible.**

1.

a. Is Sonya reading a book? ____No, she isn't.____

b. Is she talking on the phone? ________________

c. Is she eating? ________________

2.

a. Is Sam working on his car? ________________

b. Is he wearing jeans? ________________

c. Is he listening to music? ________________

3.

a. Is it snowing? ________________

b. Are they wearing T-shirts? ________________

c. Are they playing in the snow? ________________

B **Complete the questions. Use the verbs in parentheses. Then write short answers. Use contractions when possible.**

1. A: *Is* she *studying English*? (**study English**) — B: No, *she isn't*.

2. A: ________ you ________________? (**listen to music**) — B: No, ________.

3. A: ________ you ________________? (**shop for food**) — B: No, ________.

4. A: ________ it ________________ in Seattle? (**rain**) — B: Yes, ________.

5. A: ________ they ________________ today? (**go home**) — B: No, ________.

6. A: ________ it ________________ in Denver? (**snow**) — B: No, ________.

C **Complete the conversation. Use the sentences in the box.**

Great. Get matches, too.	~~No, I'm not. I'm reading a magazine.~~
Oh, good. Are you getting water?	Really?
Yes. We need good weather!	

Ann: Are you watching the news?

Tim: *No, I'm not. I'm reading a magazine.*

Ann: Well, turn on the TV. A big storm is coming.

Tim: ______________________________

Ann: Yes. In fact, I'm coming home early. I'm at the grocery store now.

Tim: ______________________________

Ann: Yes. I'm getting water, food, and a lot of batteries.

Tim: ______________________________

Ann: OK. Do we need anything else?

Tim: ______________________________

D **Play Track 44 to check your answers to Exercise C.**

A Play Track 45. Listen and read.

THE GREENVILLE CITY NEWS

The Greenville City News reporter asks this question: *What is your favorite season and why?*

Mike Stern

My favorite season is the winter. I love the cold weather. I like to play in the snow, and I like to make snowmen. And when it snows a lot, there's no school!

Darya Stern

My favorite season is the spring. I like warm weather. I don't wear a coat or a hat. I wear light clothes. And I can go for a walk after dinner.

B **Read the article again. Then choose *Mike* or *Mike's mother* for each of the statements.**

1. I love the winter.	(Mike)	Mike's mother
2. I love the spring.	Mike	Mike's mother
3. I don't have to wear a coat or hat.	Mike	Mike's mother
4. I like to play in the snow.	Mike	Mike's mother
5. I like to go for walks.	Mike	Mike's mother
6. The best part is there's no school.	Mike	Mike's mother

C **What about you? Do you like hot or cold weather? Why? Use Mike and his mother's responses as a model.**

I like ____

____

A **Look at the pictures. Complete the sentences. Use *a* or *an* when necessary.**

1. It's very cold out. You need earmuffs and gloves.

2. I need __________. It's really sunny out today.

3. It's pretty cold and rainy out. Do you have __________ and __________?

4. You need __________ when you're running. It's very sunny.

5. It's pretty cold and it's snowing. You need __________ and __________.

B **Unscramble the words to form sentences.**

1. ______________________________
   (really / hot / in / it's / and / Dallas / today / humid)

2. ______________________________
   (it's / cold / and / in / pretty / snowing / Boston / now)

3. ______________________________
   (foggy / in / San Francisco / it's / very / winter / the / in)

4. ______________________________
   (spring / weather / pretty / in / the / in / New York / nice / is / the)

C Play Track 46. Listen to the weather reports. Circle the letter of the correct answer.

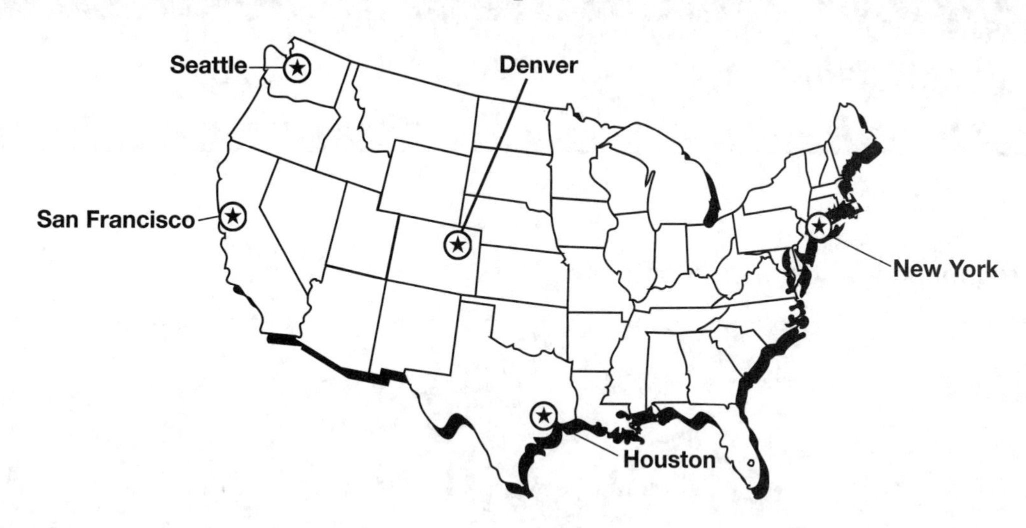

1. The weather in San Francisco is __________.

   a. cold and very foggy

   b. cool and very foggy

   c. cool but not foggy

2. The weather in Seattle is __________.

   a. rainy and pretty cool

   b. rainy and pretty cold

   c. rainy and pretty warm

3. In New York it's __________.

   a. sunny and pretty hot

   b. sunny and pretty warm

   c. sunny and very warm

4. The weather in Houston today is __________.

   a. really humid

   b. really cool

   c. really warm

5. In Denver it's __________.

   a. not very cold

   b. very cold

   c. very cool

Unit 10: Around Town

Lesson 1: Vocabulary

A **Look at the map of Watertown. Write the places.**

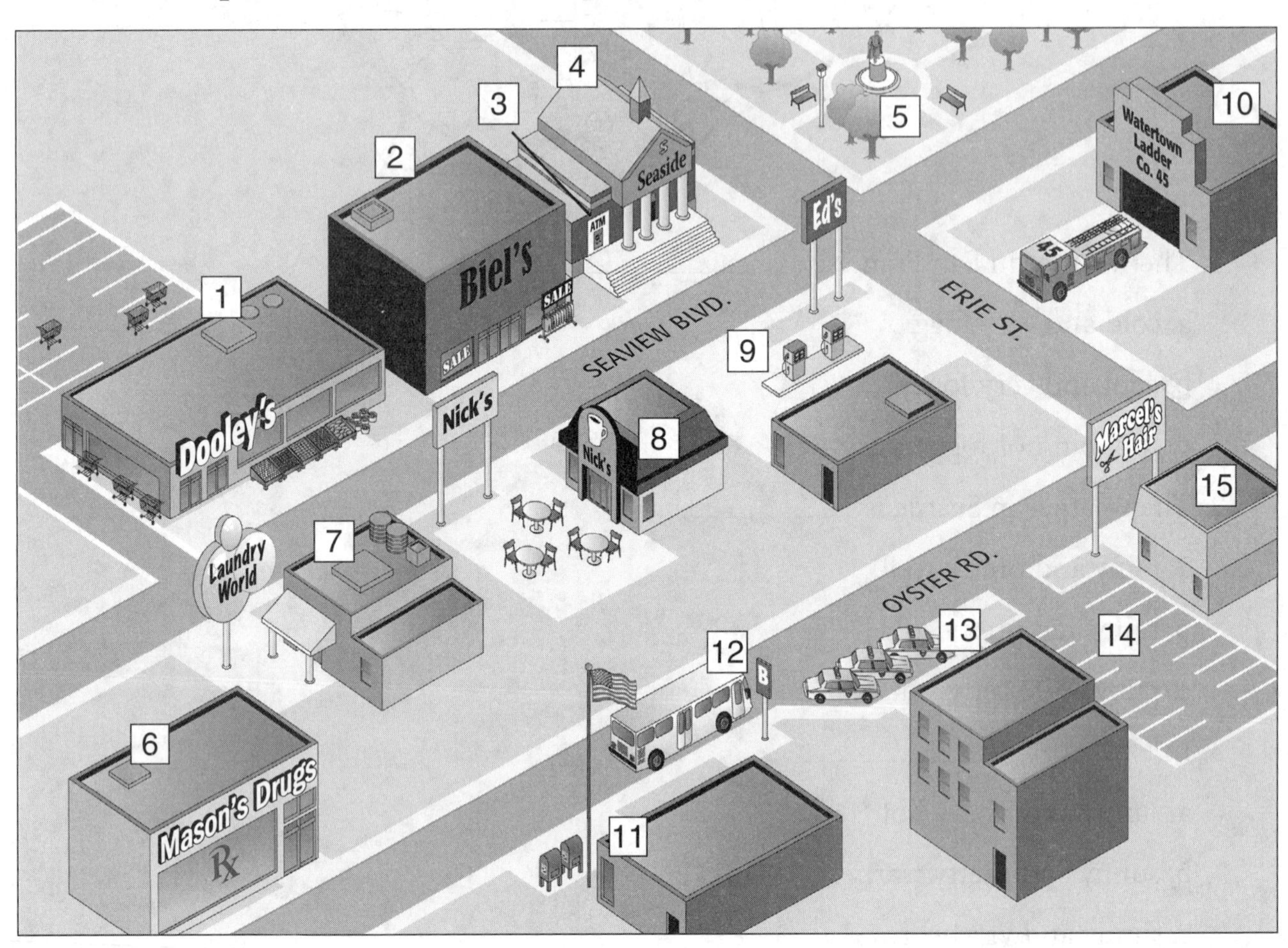

1. a supermarket
2. ______________
3. ______________
4. ______________
5. ______________
6. ______________
7. ______________
8. ______________
9. ______________
10. ______________
11. ______________
12. ______________
13. ______________
14. ______________
15. ______________

B **Look at the map in Exercise A. Complete the conversations.**

1. **A:** Is there a bank in Watertown?

   B: Yes, there is. There's a bank on Seaview Boulevard.

2. **A:** Is there a post office in Watertown?

   B: Yes, there is. There's a post office ______________________.

3. **A:** Is there a supermarket in Watertown?

   B: Yes, there is. There's a supermarket ______________________.

4. **A:** Is there a drugstore in Watertown?

   B: Yes, there is. There's a drugstore ______________________.

5. **A:** Is there a fire station in Watertown?

   B: Yes, there is. There's a fire station ______________________.

6. **A:** Is there a hair salon in Watertown?

   B: Yes, there is. There's a hair salon ______________________.

7. **A:** Is there a laundromat in Watertown?

   B: Yes, there is. There's a laundromat ______________________.

8. **A:** Is there a park in Watertown?

   B: Yes, there is. There's a park ______________________.

C **Match the sentences with the correct places.**

1. Ramon is running. c	a. the post office
2. Laura is getting money. ___	b. the drugstore
3. Mr. Lopez is picking up a package. ___	c. the park
4. Mrs. Smith is having a cup of coffee. ___	d. the supermarket
5. Carlos is buying apples. ___	e. the bank
6. Maya is getting medicine. ___	f. the coffee shop

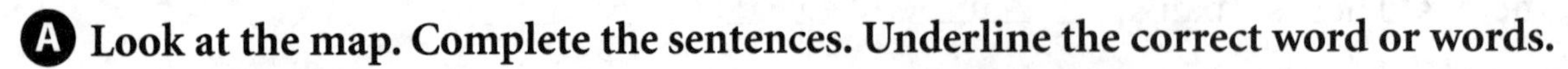

A **Look at the map. Complete the sentences. Underline the correct word or words.**

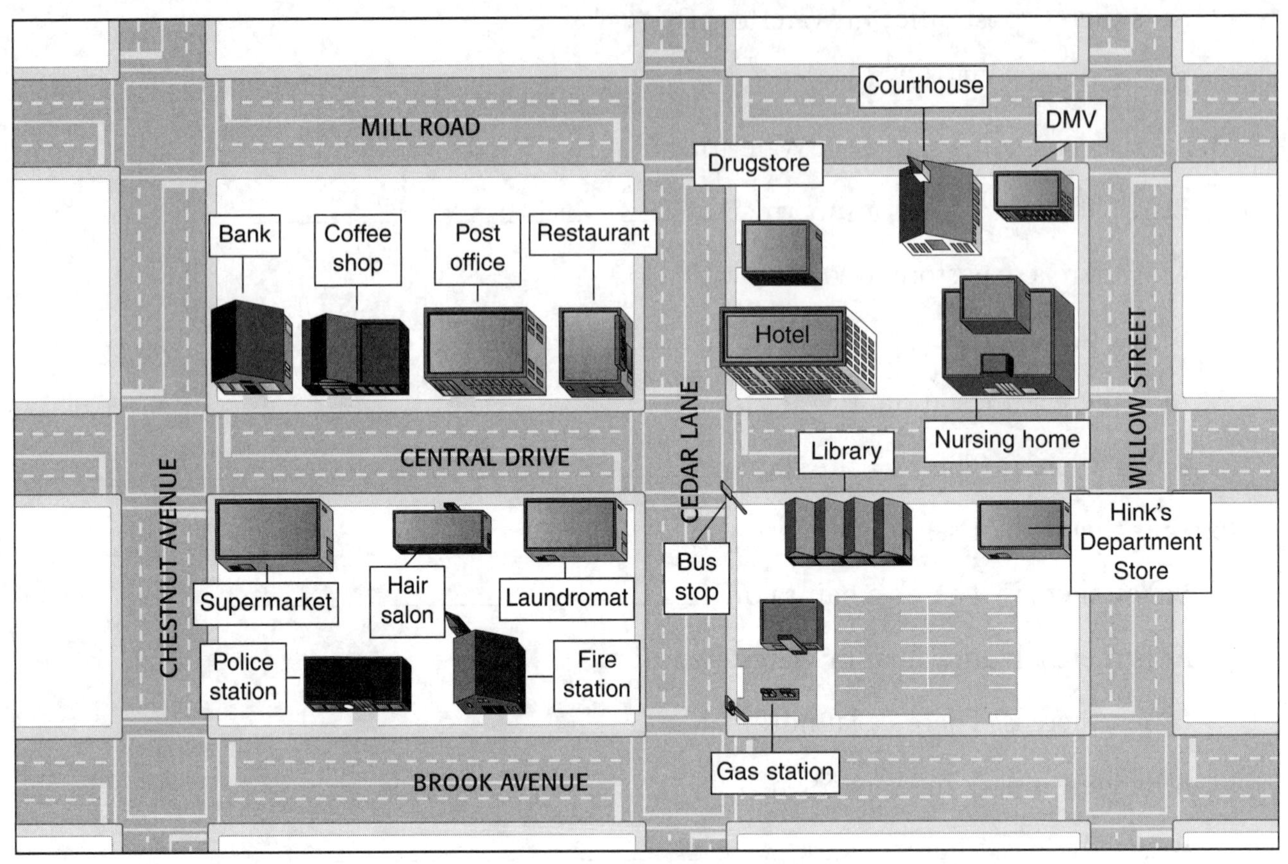

1. The post office is **on** / **near** Central Drive **between** / **next to** Chestnut Avenue and Cedar Lane.
2. The courthouse is **on** / **near** Mill Road **between** / **next to** the DMV.
3. The bank is **across from** / **next to** the coffee shop.
4. The nursing home is **across from** / **next to** Hink's Department Store.
5. The gas station is **on the corner of** / **near** Cedar Lane and Brook Avenue.
6. The supermarket is **down** / **on** the block from the laundromat.
7. The police station is **across from** / **next to** the fire station.
8. The drugstore is **around the corner** / **down the block** from the hotel.

B **Look at the map in Exercise A. Complete the sentences. Use the prepositions in the box. Some prepositions are used more than once.**

around the corner	between	down the block	near	on the corner of

1. Hink's Department Store is ___on the corner of___ Central Drive and Willow Street.
2. The post office is ______________________ the bank.
3. The hotel is ______________________ Cedar Lane and Willow Street.
4. The supermarket is ______________________ from the laundromat.
5. The bus stop is ______________________ the library.
6. The DMV is ______________________ Willow Street and Mill Road.
7. The drugstore is ______________________ from the hotel.
8. The restaurant is ______________________ from the bank.
9. The courthouse is ______________________ from the drugstore.
10. The police station is ______________________ Chestnut Avenue and Cedar Lane.

C **Look at the map in Exercise A. Read the descriptions of where the places are located. Write the names of the places.**

1. It's on Central Drive between Cedar Lane and Chestnut Avenue. It's between the bank and the post office. What is it?

   ____

2. It's across from Hink's Department Store on the corner of Willow Street. What is it?

   ____

3. It's near the laundromat and next to the hair salon. What is it?

   ____

A **Look at the pictures. Complete the conversations.**

1. 

A: How do you get to school?

B: I drive.

2. 

A: How does Monika get to school?

B: ______________________________

3. 

A: How do your children get to school?

B: ______________________________

4. 

A: How does Mrs. Martin get to school?

B: ______________________________

5. 

A: How does your brother get to work?

B: ______________________________

6. 

A: How do your parents get to work?

B: ______________________________

B Match the descriptions with the signs.

a. 

b. 

c. 

d. 

e. 

1. This sign means to drive slowly. Wait for other cars. __c__
2. This sign means you can't turn left. ____
3. This sign means there's two-way traffic. Drive on the right. ____
4. This sign means to drive slowly. People may be crossing the street. ____
5. This sign means to be ready to stop. A train may be coming. ____

C Look at the bus schedules. Complete the sentences.

RIVERSIDE BUS SCHEDULES

Bus 48		Bus 51	
14th St.	8:40	Maple Ave.	8:38
Main St.	8:52	6th Ave.	8:44
4th Ave.	8:59	8th Ave.	8:53
10th Ave.	9:06	South Dr.	9:00
Elm St.	9:12	Grand St.	9:08

1. Bus 48 leaves 14th Street at __8:40__.
2. Bus 51 leaves __Maple Avenue__ at 8:38.
3. Bus 48 leaves Main Street at ________.
4. Bus 51 leaves 6th Avenue at ________.
5. Bus 48 leaves ________ at 8:59.
6. Bus 51 leaves 8th Avenue at ________.
7. Bus 48 leaves 10th Avenue at ________.
8. Bus 51 leaves ________ at 9:00.
9. Bus 48 leaves ________ at 9:12.
10. Bus 51 leaves Grand Street at ________.

A **Complete the conversation. Use the questions in the box.**

~~How do you get to the high school?~~	How much does the train cost?
Where do you buy a ticket?	Where do you get the train?

Meg: *How do you get to the high school?*

Rob: Take the Number 12 train.

Meg: OK. ______________________

Rob: Around the corner on Colombo Road.

Meg: Great. ______________________

Rob: In the station.

Meg: Thanks. One more question. ______________________

Rob: $2.50.

B **Play Track 47 to check your answers to Exercise A.**

C **Complete the conversation. Use the questions in the box.**

How much does the bus cost?	What time does the bus leave the station?
Where do you get off?	~~Which bus goes to the high school?~~

Mark: *Which bus goes to the high school?*

Lisa: The Number 27 bus goes to the high school.

Mark: OK. ______________________

Lisa: At 7:15.

Mark: ______________________

Lisa: $3.50.

Mark: Thanks. One more question. ______________________

Lisa: Dupont Square.

D Play Track 48 to check your answers to Exercise C.

E **Complete the conversation. Make questions in the simple present. Use *How, How much,* or *Where* and add *do* or *does.***

A: ___How do___ you get to Watertown High School?

B: Take the Number 8 bus.

A: ______________ you get it?

B: At Crawford Street.

A: ______________ it cost?

B: $3.50.

A: ______________ you get off?

B: At Newport Avenue.

F **Make sentences. Use *do* or *does* and the words in parentheses.**

1. How do you get to Nick's Coffee Shop?
   (how / get / you / Nick's Coffee Shop)
2. ______________________________
   (how much / cost / the train)
3. ______________________________
   (where / get off /you)
4. ______________________________
   (where / the Number 6 bus / you / get)
5. ______________________________
   (how much / cost / the bus)
6. ______________________________
   (how / get / the library / you)
7. ______________________________
   (where / you / a ticket / the bus / for / buy)
8. ______________________________
   (how / you / the train station / get to)

Write directions

Look at the map. Your friend is staying at your home while you are away. Write directions from your house to the drugstore and to the supermarket.

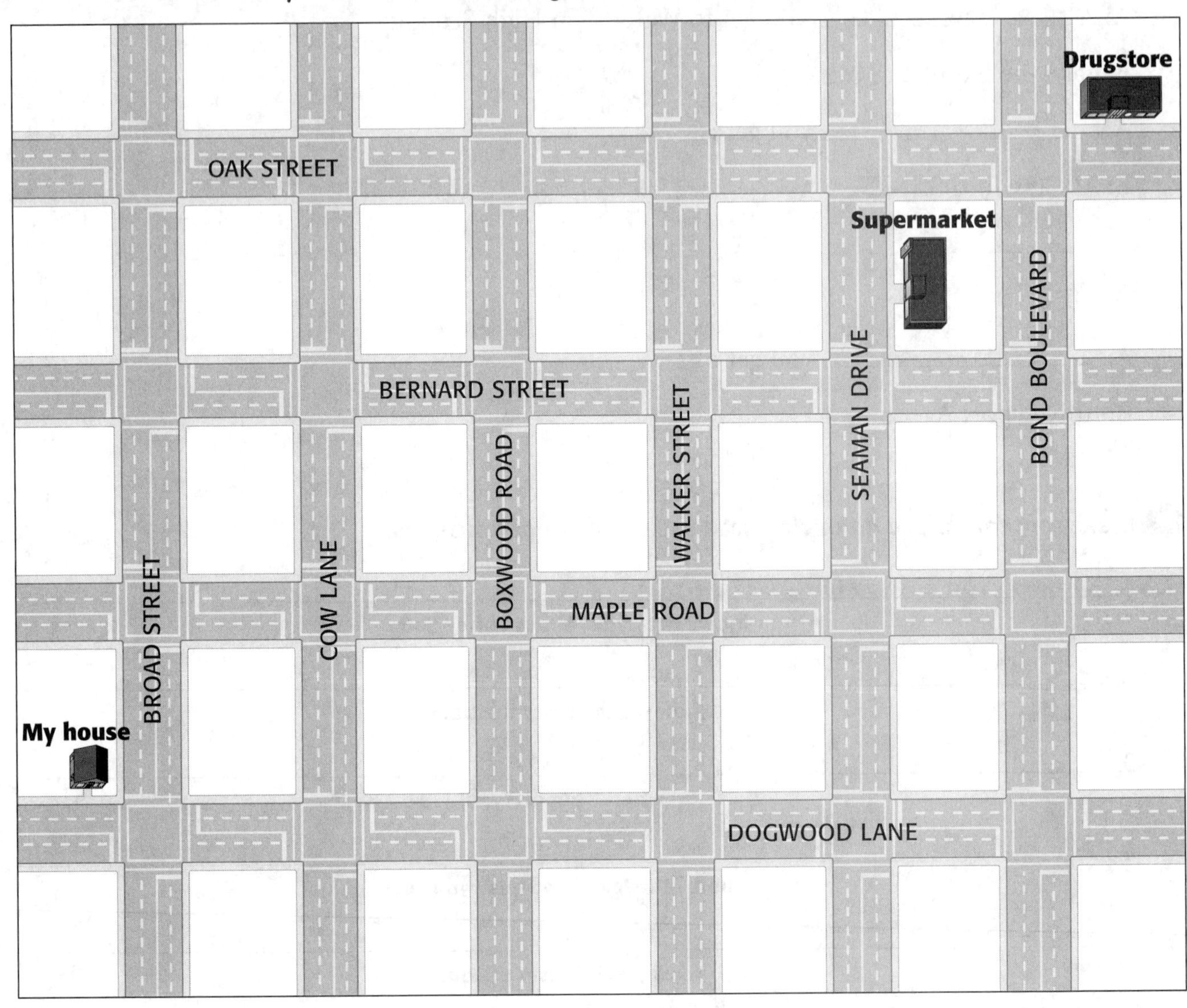

1. Directions to the drugstore: Walk down Dogwood Lane. Turn ______________________

____

2. Directions to the supermarket: ____

____

A Play Track 49. Listen and read.

THE GREENVILLE CITY NEWS

The Greenville City News reporter asks this question:
How do you get to work or school?

Omar Reyes

I work at Watertown Hospital. It's on Sutton Street downtown. I work Sundays to Thursdays. On Sundays, I drive to work because there isn't much traffic. But from Monday to Thursday I take the bus. I get on the bus down the block from my house. I get off at Sutton Street. The hospital is around the corner from the bus station.

B **Read the article again. The sentences about the article have mistakes. Correct the mistakes.**

1. Omar works at Watertown ~~Post Office~~. Hospital
2. He drives to work on Mondays.
3. From Monday to Thursday he takes the train.
4. He gets the train down the block from his house.
5. He gets off the bus at State Street.
6. The hospital is down the block from the bus station.

C **How do you get to work or school? Write about your transportation. Use Omar's response as a model.**

____

____

A **Complete the conversation. Use the present continuous tense and the verbs in parentheses. Use contractions when possible.**

A: What (do) ___are___ you ___doing___ on Saturday?

B: I (go) ______________ to a party.

A: Who (go) ______________ you ______________ with?

B: My sister (go) ______________ with me.

A: How (get) ______________ you ______________ there?

B: We (drive) ______________.

B **Look at the pictures. Ask and answer questions about the weekend. Use contractions when possible.**

1. **A:** What ___is___ Michael doing this weekend?

   B: ___He's going to a concert___ on Sunday.

2. **A:** What ______________ you doing this weekend?

   B: ______________________________ on Saturday.

3. **A:** What ______________ your sisters doing this weekend?

   B: ______________________________.

4. **A:** What ______________ Mika doing this weekend?

   B: ______________________________.

5. **A:** What ______________ Mr. Reynolds doing this weekend?

   B: ______________________________.

C Unscramble the words to form questions.

1. Where is he going this weekend?
(he / where / this / going / weekend / is)

2. ______________________________
(you / what / on / are / Saturday / doing / night)

3. ______________________________
(going / who / with / to / you / are / movies / the)

4. ______________________________
(getting / concert / to / how / sister / your / the / is)

5. ______________________________
(you / who / playing / with / are / soccer / Sunday / on)

6. ______________________________
(they / what / doing / Friday / are / night / on)

D Play Track 50. Listen to the report about events this weekend. Complete the advertisements.

Unit 11: Health Matters

Lesson 1: Vocabulary

A **Look at the picture. Write the words.**

1. head
2. ____________
3. ____________
4. ____________
5. ____________
6. ____________
7. ____________
8. ____________
9. ____________
10. ____________
11. ____________
12. ____________
13. ____________
14. ____________
15. ____________
16. ____________
17. ____________
18. ____________
19. ____________
20. ____________

B **Look at the words in the box. Put them in the correct column.**

ankle	~~ears~~	eyes	elbow	foot
hand	knee	mouth	nose	wrist

Parts of the head	Parts of the arm	Parts of the leg
ears	______	______
______	______	______
______	______	______
______		

C **Look at the pictures. Complete the sentences.**

1.  Touch your feet.

2.  Shake your ______.

3.  Nod your ______.

4.  Clap your ______.

5.  Touch your ______.

6.  Shake your ______.

Lessons 2 & 3: Talk about health problems

A **Complete the conversation. Use the correct form of *feel, have,* or *hurt.* Use contractions when possible.**

A: How ___do___ you ___feel___?

B: I __________ terrible.

A: __________ you __________ a headache?

B: No. I __________ a headache. My stomach __________.

B **Complete the sentences. Use the words in the box.**

an earache	~~the flu~~	a headache	a stomachache

1. **Martin:** I can't go to work today.
   I think I have ___the flu___.

2. **Mrs. Ramirez:** Jimmy can't go to school today.
   He has __________.

3. **Mrs. Yu:** I'm calling about my daughter. She's sick.
   She has __________.

4. **Mr. Thompson:** I'm calling about my son. He's sick.
   He has __________.

C **Look at the pictures. Complete the sentences. Use the affirmative or negative forms of *feel, have,* or *hurt.* Use contractions when possible.**

1. 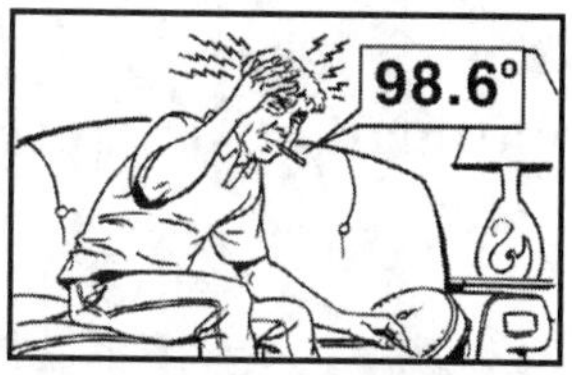 Harry ___has___ a headache.
   He ___doesn't have___ a fever.

2. 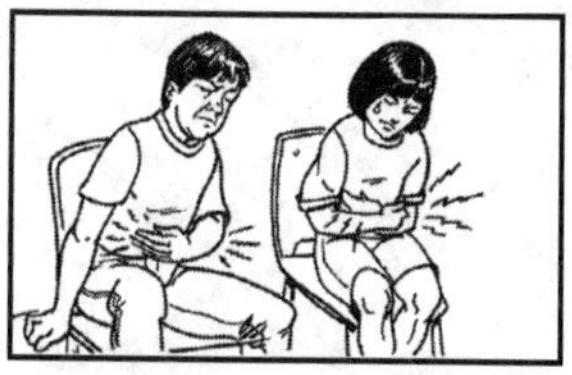 My children ____________ well.
   They ____________ stomachaches.

3.  Robert ____________ a bad toothache.
   His tooth really ____________.

4.  Jill ____________ well.
   Her head ____________.

5. 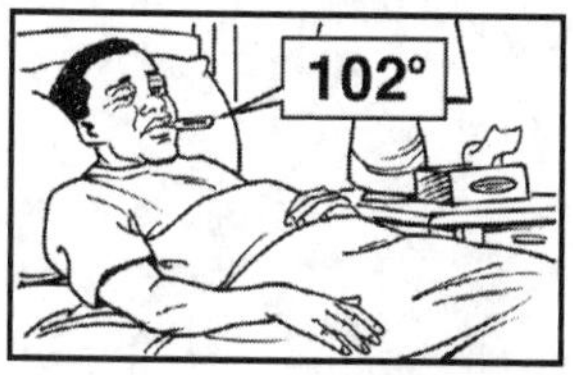 Hassan ____________ sick.
   He ____________ a fever.

6.  I ____________ well.
   I think I ____________ the flu.

D **Write questions and answers about Erica. Use the words in parentheses. Use contractions when possible.**

1. (how / Erica / feel) **A:** ___How does Erica feel?___
2. (head / hurt) **B:** ____________
3. (have / fever) **A:** ____________
4. (no / have / fever) **B:** ____________
5. (have / stuffy nose) **A:** ____________
6. (yes / have / stuffy nose) **B:** ____________

A Play Track 51. Listen to the conversation. Complete the appointment card.

You have an appointment with

Dr. Martin Russo

Primary Care Physician

On: Thursday, ______________

At: ______________ A.M. / P.M.

B Look at the appointment card. Complete the conversation.

Appointment

Children's Clinic

Alex Pietro

Date: January 31, 2009

Time: 4:30 P.M.

Mon. Tues. Wed. Thurs. (Fri.) Sat.

Assistant: Children's Clinic. Can I help you?

Mrs. Pietro: This is Mrs. Pietro. I'd like to make an appointment for my son.

Assistant: Sure. What is your son's name?

Mrs. Pietro: His name is Alex.

Assistant: Can he come in on Thursday?

Mrs. Pietro: No, I'm sorry.

Assistant: How about ______________?

Mrs. Pietro: Yes, that's good.

Assistant: Is ______________ OK?

Mrs. Pietro: Yes, we can be there.

Assistant: OK, that's ______________, ______________ at ______________. See you then.

C Complete the doctor's sentences. Use the words in the box.

lie down	open	roll up	say	sit	~~step~~	take

1. OK, Tommy, please ___step___ on the scale. How much do you weigh?
2. Now please __________ on the table.
3. OK. Now __________ your sleeve.
4. Let's see your throat. __________ your mouth and __________ "ahh."
5. And now let's check your chest. Please __________ a deep breath.
6. Now, please __________, Tommy. I'm going to check your stomach.

D Look at the medicine labels. Complete the conversations.

1. **A:** How often do I take this?

   B: Every ___6 hours___.

   A: How much do I take?

   B: You take __________.

   A: Can my son take this medicine?

   B: How old is he?

   A: He's 2.

   B: __________.

Acetafil Extra
Pain Reliever

500 mg tablets
For relief of pain from headaches, backaches, toothaches, the cold, fever

Directions:
Adults and Children 12 and older:
Take 2 tablets every 6 hours.

DO NOT TAKE MORE THAN 8 TABLETS A DAY.

DO NOT DRINK ALCOHOLIC BEVERAGES.

2. **A:** How often do I take this?

   B: Every __________.

   A: How much do I take?

   B: You take __________.

   A: Can my daughter take this medicine?

   B: How old is she?

   A: She's 12.

   B: __________.

Acetafil
Pain Reliever

250 mg tablets
For relief of pain from headaches, backaches, toothaches, the cold, fever

Directions:
Adults and Children 2 and older: Take
1 tablet every 4 hours.

DO NOT TAKE MORE THAN 4 TABLETS A DAY.

DO NOT DRINK ALCOHOLIC BEVERAGES.

Complete the form. Use true or made-up information.

PATIENT HEALTH QUESTIONNAIRE		
Name ______________________	**Date of Birth** (mm/dd/yyyy) ______________	**M** ☐ **F** ☐
Address: ______________________	**Phone:** ______________	

Please check (✓) illnesses or conditions you have now or have had in the past:

Childhood

Measles ☐	Chicken pox ☐	Mumps ☐

Adult

Asthma ☐	Tuberculosis ☐	Heart disease ☐
High Blood Pressure ☐	Diabetes ☐	HIV/AIDS ☐

Are you currently taking any medicine? Please list: ______________________ ______________________	Are you allergic to any medication? Please list: ______________________ ______________________

A Play Track 52. Listen to the sentences. Write *was, wasn't, were,* or *weren't.*

1. I ___was___ sick yesterday. I ___wasn't___ at work.
2. Carlos ________ at home last night. He ________ at his cousin's house.
3. Mari ________ absent last night. She ________ in class.
4. We ________ sick last week. We ________ in school.
5. They ________ in class yesterday. They ________ sick.

B Complete the sentences. Use the present or past tense of *be.*

1. She ___is___ at home today. She ___was___ at home yesterday, too.
2. My parents ________ in China now. They ________ in the U.S. last week.
3. We ________ back home today. We ________ in New York yesterday.
4. My sister ________ home now. She ________ in the hospital last night.
5. Alex ________ in school today. He ________ at home sick yesterday.

C Rewrite the sentences in the negative. Use *wasn't* or *weren't.*

1. Kamila was sick last night. ___Kamila wasn't sick last night.___
2. Lisa and Meg were in Peru last week. ________________
3. We were in Japan last summer. ________________
4. They were in the hospital yesterday. ________________
5. My father was sick yesterday morning. ________________

D **Look at the attendance chart. Today is Thursday. Complete the sentences about the people in class. Use *was* or *wasn't*.**

Name	Mon.	Tues.	Wed.	Thurs.	Fri.
Huang	✓	✓	A	✓	
Dominique	✓	A	✓	✓	
Rie	✓	A	✓	✓	
Yoko Mia	✓	✓	A	✓	
Carolina	A	A	A	✓	
Sibel	✓	✓	✓	A	
Alberto	✓	✓	✓	A	

1. Huang ___wasn't___ in class yesterday. She ___was___ here on Monday and Tuesday.
2. Dominique __________ here yesterday, but she __________ here on Tuesday.
3. Rie __________ here yesterday, but she __________ here the day before yesterday.
4. Yoko Mia __________ absent yesterday. She __________ here on Monday and Tuesday.
5. Carolina __________ sick this week. She __________ in school Monday, Tuesday, or Wednesday.
6. Sibel is not here today. She __________ here yesterday and the day before yesterday.
7. Alberto __________ here Monday, Tuesday, and Wednesday, but he's not here today.

E **Read the e-mail. Complete the sentences. Use *was, were, wasn't,* or *weren't*.**

I ___was___ in New York last night. I __________ at a party. It __________ a surprise party for my parents. The problem __________ that my parents __________ there. They __________ both at home. My parents __________ both sick. The surprise __________ on us! It __________ much fun without my parents.

A  **Play Track 53. Listen and read.**

THE GREENVILLE CITY NEWS

The Greenville City News reporter asks these questions: *How often do you go to the doctor? Do you go to the doctor when you're sick?*

Ramon Valdez

I don't go to the doctor very often. When I have a fever, I stay home and rest. I take an aspirin, and I drink a lot of tea. If I don't get better in a day or two, I go to the doctor.

Betty Alias

I sometimes go to the doctor. I go to the doctor when I have a fever for more than two days, and I don't feel better. Every year I go to the doctor for a checkup.

Carmela White

I don't go to the doctor very often, but I often take my kids to the clinic. When my daughter was sick last week, we were in the clinic for two hours. A lot of children were sick. The doctor was very busy.

B **Read the article again. Then complete the sentences. Underline the correct words.**

1. Ramon **goes** / **doesn't go** to the doctor often.
2. When Ramon is sick and stays home, he **drinks** / **doesn't drink** a lot of tea.
3. When Betty has a fever for more than two days she **goes** / **doesn't go** to the doctor.
4. Betty **goes** / **doesn't go** for a checkup every year.
5. Carmela **never** / **often** goes to the clinic with her children.
6. Carmela **was** / **wasn't** in the clinic last week.

C **What about you? Do you go to the doctor often? When do you go to the doctor? Use the responses above as a model.**

____

____

A Play Track 54. Listen to the conversations. Write *should* or *shouldn't.*

1. You should drink water.
2. He ________ go to school today.
3. You ________ drink a lot of juice.
4. She ________ go running.
5. She ________ drink tea and honey.
6. He ________ go to work.

B Complete the phone conversation. Use the sentences in the box.

Do you have a fever?	~~How are you? Is something wrong?~~
Oh, I'm sorry to hear that. What do you have?	You really shouldn't wait too long.
You should rest and drink a lot.	

Sara: Hi, Joe. This is Sara.

Joe: Hi, Sara. How are you? Is something wrong?

Sara: Well, I'm sick. I'm not coming to work today.

Joe: ________________________________

Sara: I'm not sure. I have a headache, and my stomach doesn't feel good.

Joe: ________________________________

Sara: Yes, I do. I just feel terrible.

Joe: Well, take it easy, Sara. ________________________________

Sara: That's a good idea.

Joe: But call the doctor if you don't feel better soon. ________________________________

Sara: OK. Thanks Joe.

C Play Track 55 to check your answers to Exercise B.

D **Look at the pictures. Complete the conversations. Give advice. Use *should* or *shouldn't* and one of the phrases in the box.**

drink milk or juice	eat a piece of onion
put butter on it	take a hot shower
take antibiotics	~~use a heating pad~~

1. 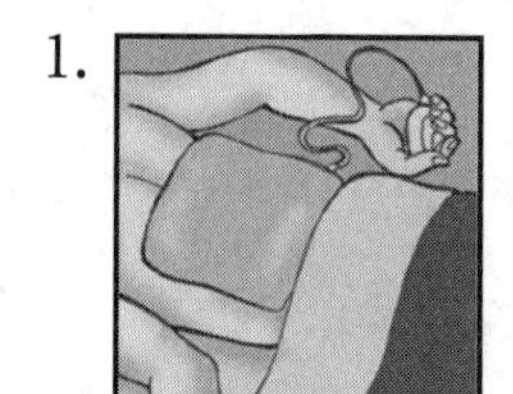

A: I have a backache.

B: I'm sorry to hear that. You _should use a heating pad_.

2. 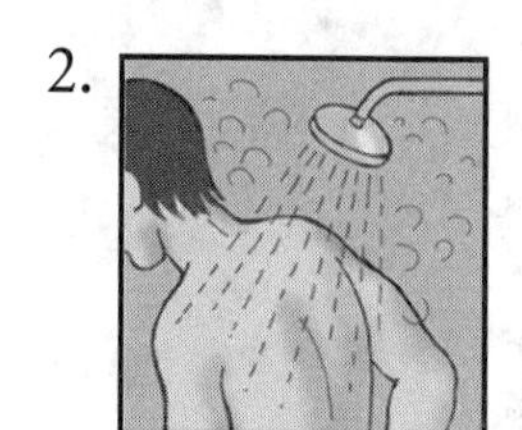

A: I have bad cold.

B: I'm sorry to hear that. You ______________________.

3. 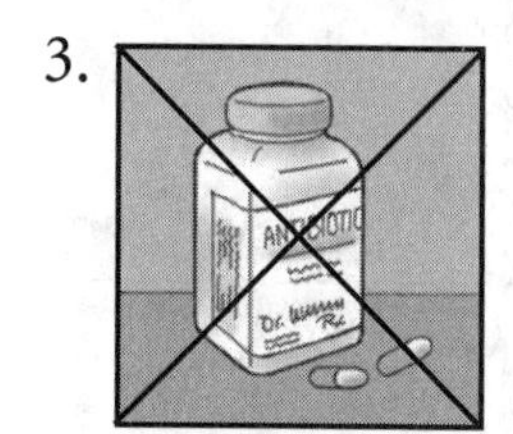

A: I have the flu.

B: You should rest. You ______________________.

4. 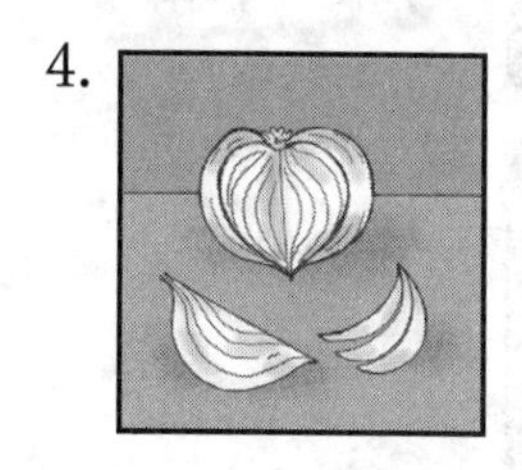

A: My tooth hurts.

B: I'm sorry to hear that. You ______________________.

5. 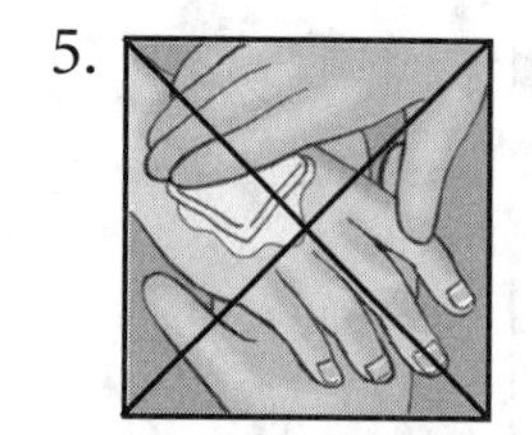

A: I have a bad burn.

B: You ______________________. You should put water on it.

6. 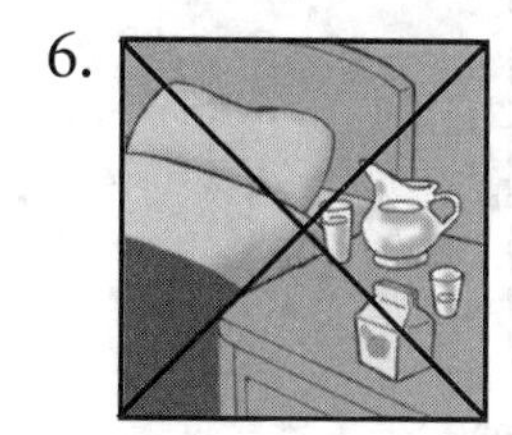

A: I have a stomachache.

B: You ______________________.

Unit 12: Help Wanted

Lesson 1: Vocabulary

A **Look at the pictures. Complete the sentences. Use the job duties in the box.**

~~answers the phone~~	delivers packages	drives a truck
helps people	takes care of grounds	uses a computer

1. An office assistant answers the phone.

2. A truck driver ______________.

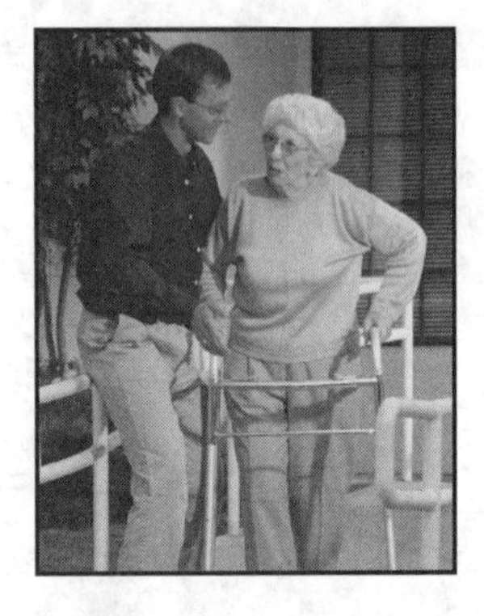

3. A caregiver ______________.

4. A gardener ______________.

5. An accountant ______________.

6. A delivery person ______________.

B **Look at the pictures. Describe what the people are doing. Write sentences. Use the words in the box. Use contractions.**

~~lifting a heavy box~~	making copies	supervising workers	taking a message

1. He's lifting a heavy box.

2. ____________________

3. ____________________

4. ____________________

C **Which word doesn't belong? Cross it out.**

1. **drive**	a truck	a car	a bus	~~a computer~~
2. **use**	a computer	a copy machine	a calculator	a message
3. **lift**	boxes	packages	furniture	rooms
4. **deliver**	mail	packages	offices	furniture
5. **clean**	floors	food	rooms	windows
6. **fix**	cars	computers	messages	copy machines

A **Complete the sentences. Use *can* and one of the verbs in the box.**

help	make	~~organize~~	speak	take	use	work	write

1. Mandy ___can organize___ things.
2. She ________________ a cash register.
3. He ________________ returns.
4. Solomon ________________ reports.
5. Alfonso ________________ with numbers.
6. Raul ________________ cabinets.
7. Karl ________________ customers.
8. Sophia ________________ English.

B **Play Track 56. Listen to the sentences. Write *can* or *can't*.**

1. Marcy has class tomorrow. She ___can't___ work.
2. Joe is a good cook. He __________ make great pizza.
3. Gwen is sick. She __________ go to class tonight.
4. I'm going to work now. I __________ drive you to school.
5. I'm good at my job. I __________ work with numbers and write reports.
6. Will is leaving the office now. He __________ pick up the package for you.
7. They're accountants. They __________ help you with your report.
8. He's a good employee, but he __________ write reports well.

C **Look at the pictures. Write sentences. Use *can* or *can't*.**

1. He can clean floors.

2. ____________________

3. ____________________

4. ____________________

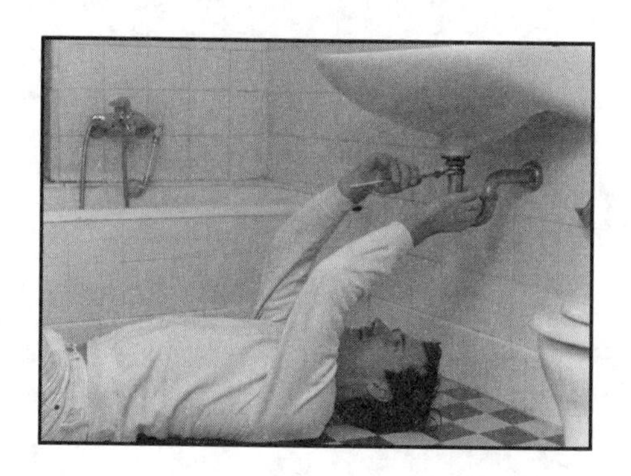

5. ____________________

6. ____________________

D **What about you? What can you do? What can't you do? Complete the sentences.**

I can ____________________.

I can't ____________________.

A Play Track 57. Listen to the phone conversation. Which ad is the man calling about? Circle the ad.

A

Office assistant

PT.
Fri–Sat 10:00 A.M.–3:00 P.M.
$12 hr.
Exp. nec.
Fax: Roberto (413) 555-3697

B

Office assistant

PT.
M–TH 9:00 A.M.–12:00 P.M.
$12 hr.
Call Mr. Rogers
(413) 555-3200

C

Office assistant

FT.
Wed–Sun 12:00–8:00 P.M.
$12 hr.
Call Devon
(413) 555-2598

B Look at the ads in Exercise A. Complete the sentences. Underline the correct words.

1. Job A is a **part-time / full-time** job.
2. Job B pays **$9 / $12** an hour.
3. Job C is a **part-time / full-time** job.
4. **Job A / Job B** is 12 hours a week.
5. You need experience for **Job A / Job C.**
6. You can call Devon about **Job B / Job C.**

C Read the descriptions about the people. Which job in Exercise A is good for them?

1. Marie can't work on weekends. Her daughter finishes school at 12:30. Job ________
2. Bob takes classes on Mondays and Tuesdays. He needs money for school. He wants to work full-time. Job ________
3. Laura has a part-time job on Mondays and Thursdays. She needs another part-time job. She has experience in an office. Job ________

D **Answer the questions about the ads.**

A

OFFICE BARN

SALES ASSISTANT
FT. Day and afternoon shifts
$8.50/hour, 40 hours/week
No experience nec.
FAX: (420) 555-8700

B

BETTER-FOR-YOU FOODS

STOCK CLERKS
PT. Afternoon and night shifts
No experience nec.
$7.00/hour
Apply in person.
850 Apple Dr.

C

RAINBOW DAYCARE

ASSISTANT CHILD-CARE WORKER

Day shift
PT. M—F, 7 to 11 A.M.
$8.00/hour
Experience with children nec.
Call Ms. O'Neil at (420) 555-7650

1. Shari wants to work at night. Which job is good for her? Job B
2. How much does the sales assistant make in one week? $340
3. Marco needs a part-time job after school. He can work in the afternoon. Which job is good for him? ____________
4. Janeen loves children. She babysits often. Which job is good for her? ____________
5. Carlo needs a full-time job. Which job is good for him? ____________
6. Frank can work in the morning. He doesn't have work experience. Which job is good for him? ____________
7. How much money does the child-care worker make in one week? ____________

E **What about you? Answer the questions. If you don't work, answer the questions with information about your school schedule.**

Do you work? ______________________________

Do you work full-time or part-time? ______________________________

How many hours do you work? ______________________________

What days do you work? ______________________________

Do you work nights? ______________________________

A **Look at the pictures. Complete the conversations. Use contractions when possible.**

1. 

A: Can they lift the stove?

B: No, they can't.

2. 

A: Can she drive a truck?

B: ______________________________

3. 

A: Can they cook?

B: ______________________________

4. 

A: Can she make furniture?

B: ______________________________

5. 

A: Can he use a cash register?

B: ______________________________

6. 

A: Can he fix computers?

B: ______________________________

B **Look at the schedule. Ask and answer questions about when the person is available to work. Use the words in parentheses.**

Sunday	Monday	Tuesday	Wednesday	Thursday	Friday	Saturday
	10–2 class	3–8 babysit Justin	10–2 class	3–8 babysit Justin	5–7 dance class	9–1 soccer

1. (Sunday mornings)

   A: Can you work on Sunday mornings? B: Yes, I can.

2. (Monday nights)

   A: ______ B: ______

3. (Tuesday nights)

   A: ______ B: ______

4. (Wednesday nights)

   A: ______ B: ______

5. (Friday nights)

   A: ______ B: ______

C **Complete the conversation. Use the questions in the box.**

Can you answer the phone?
Can you start now?
Can you use a computer?
~~OK. Which job?~~

Mia: I'm here about a job. I noticed the help wanted sign.

Yao: OK. Which job?

Mia: The cashier's job. I can use a cash register.

Yao: ______

Mia: No, I can't, but I can learn.

Yao: ______

Mia: Sure. I can answer the phone.

Yao: ______

Mia: Yes, I can.

Yao: Great! You can have the job! Welcome to Yao's Chinese Restaurant.

D Play Track 58 to check your answers to Exercise C.

A  **Play Track 59. Listen and read.**

THE GREENVILLE CITY NEWS

The Greenville City News reporter asks these questions:
Tell me about your job. What do you do? When do you work?

Christine Young

I work with computers. I do many things in my job. I fix computers. I help people with their computers. Sometimes I go to people's offices. And sometimes I go to people's homes. I work from Wednesday to Sunday.

Robert Jasinski

I work in an office. I use a computer, and I organize files. I can speak two languages: English and Spanish. I can answer the phone and help people in Spanish. I work from Monday to Friday. I can be with my family on weekends.

B Read the article again. What can they do? Check (✓) the job duties.

Christine	Use a computer __ Organize files __	Fix computers __ Speak Spanish __	Help people __ Work weekdays __	Answer the phone __ Work weekends __
Robert	Use a computer __ Organize files __	Fix computers __ Speak Spanish __	Help people __ Work weekdays __	Answer the phone __ Work weekends __

C What job duties do you have at home? What job duties do you have at work?

At home	At work
______________________	______________________
______________________	______________________
______________________	______________________

A **Complete the conversations. Use *was, wasn't, were,* or *weren't.***

1. A: ___Were___ you a student last year? B: Yes, I ___was___.
2. A: ___Was___ she a cook? B: No, she ___wasn't___.
3. A: ________ they in the United States last year? B: Yes, they ________.
4. A: ________ your brothers carpenters? B: No, they ________.
5. A: ________ it busy there? B: Yes, it ________.
6. A: How long ________ you there? B: Five years.
7. A: How long ________ Robert there? B: Two years.
8. A: How long ________ they waiters? B: Three years.
9. A: What ________ your job? B: I ________ a cashier.
10. A: What ________ her job? B: She ________ a waitress.

B **Unscramble the words to form questions.**

1. Were your parents in Colombia last year?
   (**were / in / Colombia / your parents / year / last**)
2. ________________________________
   (**long / was / she / caregiver / how / a**)
3. ________________________________
   (**they / school / were / in / yesterday**)
4. ________________________________
   (**Ms. Robles / sick / last / was / week**)
5. ________________________________
   (**nurse / you / were / a / that / in / hospital**)
6. ________________________________
   (**his / full-time / was / job**)

C **Look at Hai's job application. Complete the conversation. Use the words in parentheses.**

Name: Hai Chen

Work Experience

Name of company: Medici Accounting
345 Powers Ave.
Miami, FL 33102
Position: office assistant
From August, 2003 to September, 2005
Job Duties: answering phone, taking messages, making copies, organizing files

Name of company: Greyhound Computers
345 Lincoln Blvd.
Miami, FL 33102
Position: office assistant
From October, 2002 to July, 2003
Job Duties: answering phone, taking messages, organizing files

Joe: (office assistant) Were you an office assistant at Medici Accounting?

Hai: Yes, I was.

Joe: How long ____________________?

Hai: ____________________.

Joe: (job duties) ____________________?

Hai: ____________________.

Joe: ____________________ at Greyhound Computers also?

Hai: Yes, I was.

Joe: How long ____________________?

Hai: ____________________.

Joe: (job duties) ____________________?

Hai: ____________________.

Complete the job application. Use true or made-up information.

Computer Village

Personal Information

Last name: ______________________ First name: ______________________

Home address: ____

City: __________________ State: __________ Zip: ______________

Home phone: ________________ E-mail: ________________

Job applying for: ______________________ When can you start? __________

Are you over 18 years of age? __________ If not, date of birth: __________

Please list all the times you are available to work (from 6 A.M. to 12 A.M.)

Sun __________

M __________

T __________

W __________

Th __________

F __________

Sat __________

Education

Last school attended (name of school): ________________

Date last attended: __________

Job History (list most recent first)

Company: ______________________ Phone number: ______________

Address: ____

Job: ______________________ Dates worked: ______________

Reasons for leaving: ______________________________________

Company: ______________________ Phone number: ______________

Address: ____

Job: ______________________ Dates worked: ______________

Reasons for leaving: ______________________________________

UNIT 1

Page 5, Exercise E

Marta: Hi, I'm Marta.
Celia: Hi, Marta. I'm Celia.
Marta: Nice to meet you, Celia.
Celia: Nice to meet you, too.
Marta: Where are you from?
Celia: I'm from Brazil. What about you?
Marta: I'm from Peru.

Page 6, Exercise A

1. A: What's your first name?
   B: It's Casandra.
   A: How do you spell that?
   B: C-A-S-A-N-D-R-A.
2. A: And what's your last name?
   B: It's Balaban.
   A: How do you spell that?
   B: B-A-L-A-B-A-N.
3. A: What's your first name?
   B: It's Michael.
   A: How do you spell that?
   B: M-I-C-H-A-E-L.
4. A: And what's your last name?
   B: It's Oelbaum.
   A: How do you spell that?
   B: O-E-L-B-A-U-M.
5. A: What's your first name?
   B: It's Polina.
   A: How do you spell that?
   B: P-O-L-I-N-A.
6. A: And what's your last name?
   B: It's Sidorov.
   A: How do you spell that?
   B: S-I-D-O-R-O-V.

Page 6, Exercise B

1. A: What's your first name?
   B: My first name is Allie.
   A: How do you spell that?
   B: A-L-L-I-E.
   A: And what's your last name?
   B: Sampson.
   A: S-A-M-S-O-N?
   B: No. S-A-M-P-S-O-N.
   A: Is that Ms. or Mrs.?
   B: Ms.
2. A: Your first name, please?
   B: My first name is Rodrigo.
   A: How do you spell that?
   B: R-O-D-R-I-G-O.
   A: And what's your last name?
   B: Ferreira.
   A: How do you spell that?
   B: F-E-R-R-E-I-R-A.
   A: Thank you.
3. A: Can you tell me your first name, please?
   B: My first name is Svetlana.
   A: How do you spell that?
   B: S-V-E-T-L-A-N-A.
   A: And what's your last name?
   B: Jones.
   A: J-O-N-E-S?
   B: Yes.
   A: Is that Ms. or Mrs.?
   B: Mrs.

Page 13, Exercise E

Rob: Who's that?
Ana: That's the teacher.
Sue: That's not the teacher.
Ana: You're right. That's Mila.
Rob: Where's she from?
Ana: She's from Russia. She's in level 1.
Rob: Who's that?
Ana: That's Juan.
Sue: That's not Juan.
Ana: You're right. That's Mr. Jones.
Rob: Where's he from?
Ana: He's from the United States. He's the teacher. He's great.

UNIT 2

Page 17, Exercise D

Mike: Sonia, this is Marie. Marie, this is Sonia.
Sonia: Hi, Marie. It's nice to meet you.
Marie: Nice to meet you, too, Sonia.
Sonia: So, Marie, what do you do?
Marie: I'm an office assistant. What about you?
Sonia: I'm an office assistant, too.
Marie: Oh, that's interesting.

Page 18, Exercise A

1. three
2. six
3. eight
4. one
5. zero
6. nine
7. five
8. seven
9. four
10. two

Page 18, Exercise C

1. (903) 555-3460
2. (302) 555-6092
3. (903) 555-8416
4. (302) 555-7981
5. (302) 555-8132

Page 19, Exercise E

1. A: Directory Assistance.
   B: What's the number for The Blue Moon Restaurant?
   A: The number is (473) 555-3442.
   B: Thank you.
2. A: Directory Assistance.
   B: What's the number for Kay's Clothes Store?
   A: The number is (473) 555-8976.
   B: Thank you.
3. A: Directory Assistance.
   B: What's the number for Mountainville Hospital?
   A: The number is (473) 555-7840.
   B: Thank you.
4. A: Directory Assistance.
   B: What's the number for The Peamont Child-Care Center?
   A: The number is (473) 555-4738.
   B: Thank you.
5. A: Directory Assistance.
   B: What's the number for Shelburn Office Supplies?
   A: The number is (473) 555-9267.
   B: Thank you.

Page 19, Exercise F

1. This is Mr. Lee. I'm calling about the waiter job. Please call me back at (897) 555-0232. That's (897) 555-0232.
2. This is Monica Hempler. I'm calling about the gardener job. Please call me back at (679) 555-7861. That's (679) 555-7861.
3. This is Ms. Peterson. I'm calling about the accountant job. My number is (416) 555-5267. That's (416) 555-5267.
4. This is Carlos Rivera. I'm calling about the office assistant job. My number is (347) 555-4568. That's (347) 555-4568.

Page 22, Exercise C

1. A: What does Calvin do?
   B: He's a cook.
2. A: What does Ms. Torres do?
   B: She's a child-care worker.
3. A: What does Hong-Yi do?
   B: He's an electrician.
4. A: What does Kristina do?
   B: She's an accountant.
5. A: What does Daniel do?
   B: He's an office assistant.
6. A: What does Elena do?
   B: She's an accountant.
7. A: What does Rodrigo do?
   B: He's an artist.
8. A: What does Kim do?
   B: She's a child-care worker.
9. A: What does Robert do?
   B: He's a cook.

Page 24, Exercise C

a. She works in a restaurant. She's a cook.
b. She works in a store. She's a stock clerk.
c. He works in a nursing home. He's a caregiver.
d. She works at a factory. She's an assembly-line worker.

Page 25, Exercise F

Edna: Hi, I'm Edna.
Sam: Hi, Edna. I'm Sam.
Edna: It's nice to meet you.
Sam: It's nice to meet you, too.
Edna: Are you a student here?
Sam: No, I'm not. I'm a teacher.
Edna: Really? That's interesting.
Sam: What do you do, Edna?
Edna: I'm an artist.
Sam: Really? Where do you work?
Edna: I work in Boston.
Sam: That's great!

UNIT 3

Page 33, Exercise D

1. Is this a monitor?
2. Is that a keyboard?
3. Is this a binder?
4. Are these folders?
5. Is this a DVD?
6. Are those CDs?

Page 34, Exercise C

1. A: What room is the cafeteria?
   B: It's Room 17.
2. A: What room is the computer lab?
   B: It's Room 23.

3. A: What room is the library?
   B: It's Room 28.
4. A: What room is the main office?
   B: It's Room 19.

Page 36, Exercise B

1. A: Where's the office?
   B: I don't know. That's Ms. Kramer. She's the principal. Ask her.
2. A: Where's the elevator?
   B: I don't know. That's Mr. Yu. He's the custodian. Ask him.
3. A: Is the library upstairs?
   B: I don't know. That's Mrs. Cowalski. She's the librarian. Ask her.
4. A: Is the computer lab open?
   B: I don't know. That's Paulo. He's the computer lab assistant. Ask him.
5. A: Where's the ESL office?
   B: I don't know. That's Miss White. She's the office assistant. Ask her.

Page 37, Exercise F

Bob: Excuse me. Can you help me?
Meg: Sure.
Bob: What room is the ESL office?
Meg: Sorry. I don't know. Ask him.
Bob: Uh . . . who's he?
Meg: That's Mr. Smith, the custodian.
Bob: Excuse me. Which way is the ESL office?
Mr. Smith: It's down the hall on the left, Room 24.
Bob: Thank you.
Mr. Smith: You're welcome.

UNIT 4

Page 41, Exercise F

Eva: That's a great photo. Who's that?
Tom: That's my sister, Fran.
Eva: She looks nice. Is that your mother?
Tom: Yes, it is.
Eva: Fran looks like her.
Tom: Yes. And this is my brother, Tim.
Eva: He looks like your mother, too.
Tom: I know. And I look like my father.

Page 44, Exercise F

Mary: Is your family here in this country?
Luz: Well, my brother and sister are here. My parents are in Mexico.
Mary: What's your brother like?
Luz: He's great.
Mary: Does he look like you?
Luz: Yes. He's tall and thin and has short hair.
Mary: What about your sister? Does she look like you?
Luz: No. She's average height and heavy. She has long hair.

Page 45, Exercise A

A: Hi, James. We have a busy month in February.
B: Yes, I know. We have five family birthdays. Judy's birthday is on the fifth.
A: Right. And your brother Randy's is on the ninth. But when is Kevin's birthday?
B: It's the fifteenth.
A: And then Martha's is the nineteenth.
B: And don't forget my birthday. It's the twenty-fourth.
A: Oh, sorry!

Page 46, Exercise D

1. May fourth, two thousand and four
2. October eighth, nineteen eighty-three
3. January seventh, nineteen ninety-nine
4. September twenty-sixth, two thousand and three
5. July twenty-eighth, nineteen fifty-two
6. May thirteenth, nineteen ninety-five
7. March twelfth, two thousand and seven
8. April ninth, nineteen seventy-four

Page 47, Exercise B

A: How old are your children?
B: I have two boys and a girl. My son, José, is 14. He's in the ninth grade.
A: OK. So he's in the ninth grade.
B: Yes. Then, Carmen is 11.
A: So, she's in the fifth grade?
B: No. She's in the sixth grade.
A: Sorry. The sixth grade. And your third child? How old is he?
B: Miguel is eight. He's in the third grade.

Page 48, Exercise F

Mark: Hi, Nina. Where are you?
Nina: I'm at my cousin's house. I'm babysitting for her kids.
Mark: Oh, that's nice. How old are they?
Nina: Well, her daughter is nine. She's in the fourth grade. And her son is seven. He's in the second grade.

UNIT 5

Page 55, Exercise F

1. A: How much is the blouse?
   B: It's $24.95.
2. A: How much are the shoes?
   B: They're $37.50.
3. A: How much is the T-shirt?
   B: It's $14.99.
4. A: How much are the socks?
   B: They're $9.95.
5. A: How much is the wallet?
   B: It's $34.50.
6. A: How much are the pants?
   B: They're $49.99.

Page 58, Exercise D

Mother: Linda, look at the sale! Do you need clothes for school?
Linda: Yes, I do. I need T-shirts.
Mother: Well, they have T-shirts in green, yellow, and blue.
Linda: I like the blue T-shirts.
Mother: You need black pants. Do they have them?
Linda: Yes, they do. I like these black pants.
Mother: Do they have a small?
Linda: Yes, they do. Here they are.
Mother: And the jackets are great. You need a new jacket, too. Do you like this jacket?
Linda: No, I don't.
Mother: OK.

UNIT 6

Page 65, Exercise C

1. There's an old kitchen.
2. There's a sunny bedroom.
3. It's a cheap house.
4. There's a large bathroom.

Page 69, Exercise A

1. 365 Meadow Drive
2. 52 Park Boulevard
3. 45 Orange Avenue
4. 37 Sutton Street
5. 145 Drake Road

Page 70, Exercise E

1. A: Is there a one-bedroom apartment available?
   B: Yes, there is.
   A: How much is it?
   B: It's $1,200 a month.
   A: Does it have a new kitchen?
   B: No, it doesn't, but it has a large kitchen with a new stove.
   A: Does it have parking?
   B: Yes, it has parking.
   A: What's the address?
   B: It's 14 Bank Street, Apartment 3D.
2. A: Is there a two-bedroom apartment available?
   B: Yes, there is.
   A: How much is it?
   B: It's $1,300 a month.
   A: Does it have a large bathroom?
   B: Yes, it does. It has a large bathroom with a new shower.
   A: Are utilities included?
   B: Yes, they are.
   A: What's the address?
   B: It's 346 Clover Boulevard, Apartment 1C.
3. A: Is there a three-bedroom apartment for rent?
   B: Yes, there is. And the building is new.
   A: How much is it?
   B: It's $1,450 a month.
   A: Does it have a dining room?
   B: Yes, there's a large dining room.
   A: What's the address?
   B: 45 Orchard Avenue, Apartment 2B.
4. A: Is there a one-bedroom apartment for rent?
   B: Yes, there is.
   A: How much is it?
   B: It's $900 a month.
   A: Is there a dining room?
   B: No, but there's a large living room.
   A: Does it have laundry and parking?
   B: It doesn't have parking. But there's a laundry room in the building.
   A: What's the address?
   B: 3 Apple Drive, Apartment 2A.

Page 73, Exercise D

Go north on Powell Street. Continue on Powell Street for three blocks. Turn right at the 2nd light. Continue east on Starrett Street. Our store is on Starrett Street on the right. It's at 3228 Starrett Street.

UNIT 7

Page 78, Exercise A

A: Hi, Marie. Are you free for lunch any day this week?
B: Gee, I'm not sure. I have a very busy schedule this week.
A: Well, how about Tuesday?
B: Oh, no, sorry. You know, I work on Tuesdays and Thursdays from 10:00 to 2:00.

A: Oh, too bad. How about Wednesday?
B: Oh, no, sorry. On Wednesdays I have English class from 1:00 to 5:00. Oh, wait. Friday is good. I'm free on Friday!

Page 85, Exercise B

A: So, Ms. Jones, can you tell us what activities you do to relax?
B: Well, I exercise.
A: Really? How often do you exercise?
B: I go running three times a week.
A: Great!
B: And I take a long walk once a week.
A: Oh, that's good.
B: And I do puzzles.
A: How often do you do puzzles?
B: Every day. I love puzzles.
A: Great. What about music? How often do you listen to music?
B: Oh, never. I never listen to music.

UNIT 8

Page 93, Exercise D

A: Can I help you?
B: Yes, I'd like to order a green salad.
A: OK.
B: I'd like a hamburger, too.
A: OK. A green salad and a hamburger. Anything else?
B: Yes, please. An order of fries.
A: Large or small?
B: Large, please.
A: Anything to drink?
B: Yes, a large soda.
A: OK. And what would you like, sir?
C: I'd like a bowl of soup.
A: A bowl of soup. OK. Anything else?
C: A chicken sandwich and a baked potato, please.
A: A chicken sandwich and a baked potato. OK. Would you like anything to drink?
C: A large iced tea, please.
A: OK. Anything else?
C: Oh, yes. Apple pie.
A: Apple pie. OK.

Page 95, Exercise C

Welcome shoppers. Today at Foodmart we have specials in every department. This week only we have green beans on sale for just $1.19 a pound. That's right—just $1.19 a pound. We also have potatoes on sale for just 79¢ a pound. In our fish and seafood department we have fresh fish for just $3.99 a pound. And in our meat department we have chicken on sale for just $3.59 a pound. And go to our bakery to find bread on sale for $2.99. Thanks for shopping at Foodmart this week.

Page 97, Exercise C

A: Let's have grilled chicken and rice.
B: And I can make a large green salad.
A: Yes, and for drinks, we can serve water, juice, and soda.
B: That sounds good. What else do we need?
A: A dessert? Can you make apple pie?
B: Sure. I'll make two apple pies.

UNIT 9

Page 103, Exercise B

A: We need to get some things for the storm.
B: Yeah, we do. We don't have candles.
A: Oh, you're right. And we need matches, too.
B: OK. Hmm. What about water? Do we have bottles of water?
A: Uh, not many. Let's buy two or three more.
B: All right. We need a new flashlight also.
A: OK. And don't forget batteries.

Page 106, Exercise D

Ann: Are you watching the news?
Tim: No, I'm not. I'm reading a magazine.
Ann: Well, turn on the TV. A big storm is coming.
Tim: Really?
Ann: Yes. In fact, I'm coming home early. I'm at the grocery store now.
Tim: Oh, good. Are you getting water?
Ann: Yes. I'm getting water, food, and a lot of batteries.
Tim: Great. Get matches, too.
Ann: OK. Do we need anything else?
Tim: Yes. We need good weather!

Page 109, Exercise C

1. In San Francisco it's cool and very foggy today.
2. In Seattle it's rainy and pretty cool—only 58°.
3. It's a beautiful day in New York. It's sunny and pretty warm for March—72°.
4. It's another hot and humid day in Houston. It's really humid and the temperature is already 86°.
5. Denver has perfect weather for making snowmen. It's not snowing, but it's very cold—18°.

UNIT 10

Page 116, Exercise B

Meg: How do you get to the high school?
Rob: Take the Number 12 train.
Meg: OK. Where do you get the train?
Rob: Around the corner on Colombo Road.
Meg: Great. Where do you buy a ticket?
Rob: In the station.
Meg: Thanks. One more question. How much does the train cost?
Rob: $2.50.

Page 117, Exercise D

Mark: Which bus goes to the high school?
Lisa: The Number 27 bus goes to the high school.
Mark: OK. What time does the bus leave the station?
Lisa: At 7:15.
Mark: How much does the bus cost?
Lisa: $3.50.
Mark: Thanks. One more question. Where do you get off?
Lisa: Dupont Square.

Page 121, Exercise D

There are plenty of fun things happening in our area this weekend. There's a new movie opening at the Howlie Theater. *Sands of Time* has shows on Friday and Saturday night at 7:30, 9:50, and 11:15. If it's sports you're after, the Vikings are playing soccer at the high school on Sunday afternoon. The game starts at 3 P.M. If you like rock music, the Heavenly Six are playing in town on Saturday night. The concert begins at 8 P.M.

UNIT 11

Page 126, Exercise A

Cathy: Good morning. Dr. Russo's office. This is Cathy.
Lucy: Hi, Cathy. This is Lucy Peterson. I'd like to make an appointment with Dr. Russo.
Cathy: Sure. What day?
Lucy: Does he have anything on Wednesday?
Cathy: Hmm. No, I'm sorry. How about Thursday morning?
Lucy: OK. Thursday morning is good. What time?
Cathy: How's 10:30?
Lucy: That's fine.
Cathy: OK. That's Thursday, May 14th, at 10:30. See you then.

Page 129, Exercise A

1. I was sick yesterday. I wasn't at work.
2. Carlos wasn't at home last night. He was at his cousin's house.
3. Mari wasn't absent last night. She was in class.
4. We were sick last week. We weren't in school.
5. They weren't in class yesterday. They were sick.

Page 132, Exercise A

1. A: I have a bad headache.
   B: You should drink water.
2. A: He has the flu.
   B: He shouldn't go to school today.
3. A: We have colds.
   B: You should drink a lot of juice.
4. A: Ms. Moyer has a backache.
   B: She shouldn't go running.
5. A: She has a bad cough.
   B: She should drink tea and honey.
6. A: Mr. Moore has a fever.
   B: He shouldn't go to work.

Page 132, Exercise C

Sara: Hi, Joe. This is Sara.
Joe: Hi, Sara. How are you? Is something wrong?
Sara: Well, I'm sick. I'm not coming to work today.
Joe: Oh, I'm sorry to hear that. What do you have?
Sara: I'm not sure. I have a headache, and my stomach doesn't feel good.
Joe: Do you have a fever?
Sara: Yes, I do. I just feel terrible.
Joe: Well, take it easy, Sara. You should rest and drink a lot.
Sara: That's a good idea.
Joe: But call the doctor if you don't feel better soon. You really shouldn't wait too long.
Sara: OK. Thanks Joe.

UNIT 12

Page 136, Exercise B

1. Marcy has class tomorrow. She can't work.
2. Joe is a good cook. He can make great pizza.
3. Gwen is sick. She can't go to class tonight.
4. I'm going to work now. I can't drive you to school.
5. I'm good at my job. I can work with numbers and write reports.
6. Will is leaving the office now. He can pick up the package for you.
7. They're accountants. They can help you with your report.
8. He's a good employee, but he can't write reports well.

Page 138, Exercise A

A: Colony Real Estate. How can I help you?
B: I'm calling about the ad in the paper today.
A: Which ad?
B: The ad for an office assistant.
A: Oh, yes. Do you have office experience?
B: Yes, I do. And the hours are on Fridays and Saturdays?
A: Yes. Fridays and Saturdays from 10 to 3.
B: And it pays $12 an hour?
A: Yes, that's right. Can you use a computer?
B: Yes, I can use a computer.
A: Great! Why don't you come in this afternoon at 3:00?
B: OK. Thanks.

Page 141, Exercise D

Mia: I'm here about a job. I noticed the Help Wanted sign.
Yao: OK. Which job?
Mia: The cashier's job. I can use a cash register.
Yao: Can you use a computer?
Mia: No, I can't. But I can learn.
Yao: Can you answer the phone?
Mia: Sure. I can answer the phone.
Yao: Can you start now?
Mia: Yes, I can.
Yao: Great! You can have the job! Welcome to Yao's Chinese Restaurant.

Answer Key

UNIT 1

Page 2, Exercise A

1. The United States
2. Mexico
3. Canada
4. Peru
5. Haiti
6. Brazil
7. El Salvador
8. England
9. Poland
10. Somalia
11. China
12. Korea
13. Russia
14. Ethiopia
15. Vietnam

Page 3, Exercise B

1. Canada
2. The United States
3. Mexico
4. Haiti
5. El Salvador
6. Peru
7. Brazil
8. England
9. Poland
10. Ethiopia
11. Somalia
12. Russia
13. China
14. Korea
15. Vietnam

Page 4, Exercise A

1. I'm from Poland.
2. I'm from El Salvador.
3. I'm from Vietnam.
4. I'm from England.
5. I'm from Ethiopia.
6. I'm from Korea.

Page 4, Exercise B

1. is from Poland
2. is from El Salvador
3. is from Vietnam
4. is from England
5. is from Ethiopia
6. is from Korea

Page 5, Exercise C

4 Nice to meet you, too.
2 Hi, Marta. I'm Celia.
3 Nice to meet you, Celia.
5 Where are you from?
6 I'm from Brazil. What about you?
1 Hi, I'm Marta.
7 I'm from Peru.

Page 5, Exercise D

Marta: Hi, I'm Marta.
Celia: Hi, Marta. I'm Celia.
Marta: Nice to meet you, Celia.
Celia: Nice to meet you, too.
Marta: Where are you from?
Celia: I'm from Brazil. What about you?
Marta: I'm from Peru.

Page 5, Exercise F

Answers will vary.

Page 6, Exercise A

1. Casandra
2. Balaban
3. Michael
4. Oelbaum
5. Polina
6. Sidorov

Page 6, Exercise B

1.

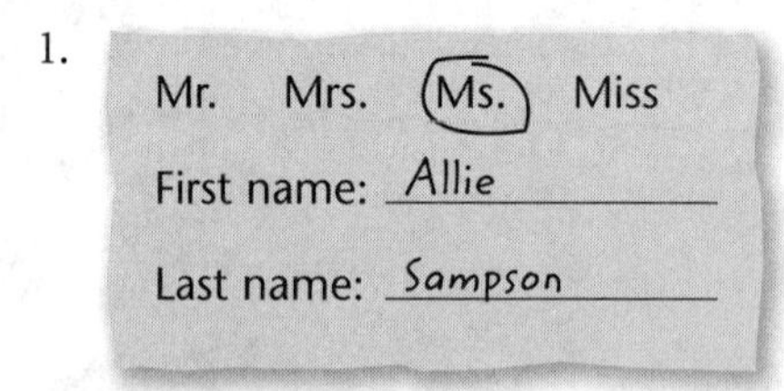

Mr. Mrs. (Ms.) Miss
First name: Allie
Last name: Sampson

2.

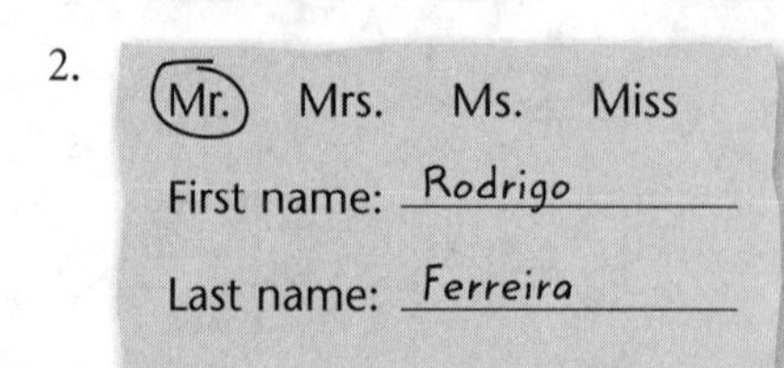

(Mr.) Mrs. Ms. Miss
First name: Rodrigo
Last name: Ferreira

3.

Mr. (Mrs.) Ms. Miss
First name: Svetlana
Last name: Jones

Page 7, Exercise C

Briet, Monica
Kim, Jai-Soo
Lee, Yu-Min
Montana, Sandra
Salder, George
Tran, Nyet
Vasquez, Antonio

Page 7, Exercise D

Cardoso, Pedro
Castillo, Rafael
Cheban, Moriz
Chiang, Yao
Chong, Chun-Mei
Colombo, Angela
Conklin, Marta

Page 7, Exercise E

Abrams, Molly
Dols, Elaine
Mendez, Carla
Monro, Guy
Ribeiro, Tania
Rivera, Joel
Sun, Li

Page 8, Exercise A

Please print. Use blue or black ink.
Name: Juevez (LAST) Bonita (FIRST) Marie (MIDDLE)
☐ Male ☑ Female
Signature: Bonita Juevez

Page 8, Exercise B

Answers will vary.

Page 8, Exercise C

1. My first name is Darya.
2. My last name is Ivanova.
3. I'm from Ecuador.
4. I'm married.

Page 9, Exercise A

1. am / am 2. is / is 3. is / is

Page 9, Exercise B

1. She is from Peru.
2. He is from Mexico.
3. He is from the United States.
4. She is from Korea.

Page 9, Exercise C

1. She's
2. He's
3. She's
4. He's

Page 10, Exercise D

1. Katya isn't in level 2. She's in level 1.
2. José isn't from El Salvador. He's from Mexico.
3. She isn't from Canada. She's from Russia. OR She's not from Canada. She's from Russia.
4. Mr. Fanelli isn't the teacher. He's a student.
5. I'm not in level 3. I'm in level 1.

Page 10, Exercise E

1. Ms. Cabral isn't from China. She's from Brazil.
2. Mr. Duval isn't in Level 2. He's in Level 1.
3. Mrs. Gao isn't from Haiti. She's from China.
4. Mr. Medina isn't from Brazil. He's from Mexico.
5. Mr. Motalev isn't in Level 2. He's in Level 3.
6. Ms. Park isn't in Level 3. She's in Level 2.

Page 11, Exercise B

1. True
2. True
3. True
4. False
5. False

Page 11, Exercise C

Answers will vary.

Page 12, Exercise A

1. are / They're in level 2.
2. are / We're students.
3. are / You're a student.
4. are / Lev and I are from Russia.
5. are / Marta and Ilhan are in level 3.
6. is / It's interesting.

Page 12, Exercise B

1. We are from El Salvador.
2. We are in level 2.
3. Tomas and Celia are from Brazil.
4. You are a student.
5. Tania and I are absent today.

Page 12, Exercise C

1. d 2. c 3. b 4. a

Page 13, Exercise D

1. They aren't in level 4. OR They're not in level 4.
2. We aren't from Somalia. OR We're not from Somalia.
3. My English class isn't hard.
4. Mr. and Mrs. Kim aren't from China.
5. Celia and I aren't students.
6. Calvin and Ricardo aren't from El Salvador.
7. Diego and Armando aren't students.
8. This book isn't interesting.

Page 13, Exercise E

Rob: Who's that?
Ana: That's *the teacher*.
Sue: That's *not* the teacher.
Ana: You're right. That's Mila.
Rob: Where's *she* from?
Ana: *She's* from Russia. *She's* in level 1.
Rob: Who's that?
Ana: That's Juan.
Sue: That's *not* Juan.
Ana: You're right. That's Mr. Jones.
Rob: Where's *he* from?
Ana: *He's* from the United States. *He's* the teacher. *He's* great.

UNIT 2

Page 14, Exercise A

1. sales assistant
2. gardener
3. homemaker
4. artist
5. driver
6. nurse
7. child-care worker
8. doctor
9. housekeeper

Page 14, Exercise B

1. sales assistant
2. driver
3. doctor
4. artist
5. homemaker
6. child-care worker
7. gardener
8. housekeeper
9. nurse

Page 15, Exercise C

1. doctor
2. cashier
3. waitress
4. cook

Page 15, Exercise D

1. accountant
2. painter
3. office assistant
4. electrician

Page 16, Exercise A

1. a 2. an 3. a 4. a 5. a 6. an 7. a 8. an

Page 17, Exercise B

1. Paul and Rafael are doctors.
2. Carla and Lucia are waitresses.
3. Marco and Tania are nurses.
4. Liam and Sal are gardeners.
5. Mia and Luz are artists.
6. Kim and Mike are cashiers.

Page 17, Exercise C

Mike: Sonia, this is Marie. Marie, this is Sonia.
Sonia: Hi, Marie. It's nice to meet you.
Marie: Nice to meet you too, Sonia.
Sonia: So, Marie, what do you do?
Marie: I'm an office assistant. What about you?
Sonia: I'm an office assistant, too.
Marie: Oh, that's interesting.

Page 18, Exercise A

1. 3	6. 9
2. 6	7. 5
3. 8	8. 7
4. 1	9. 4
5. 0	10. 2

Page 18, Exercise B

1. three
2. six
3. eight
4. one
5. zero
6. nine
7. five
8. seven
9. four
10. two

Page 18, Exercise C

1. d 2. c 3. b 4. a 5. e

Page 19, Exercise D

1. (212) 555-3480
2. (718) 555-9322
3. (631) 555-1871
4. (914) 555-4438

Page 19, Exercise E

The Blue Moon Restaurant: (473) 555-3442
Kay's Clothes Store: (473) 555-8976
Mountainville Hospital: (473) 555-7840
The Peamont Child-Care Center: (473) 555-4738
Shelburn Office Supplies: (473) 555-9267

Page 19, Exercise F

1. Call Mr. Lee about the waiter job at (897) 555-0232.
2. Call Monica Hempler about the gardener job at (679) 555-7861.
3. Call Ms. Peterson about the accountant job at (416) 555-5267.
4. Call Carlos Rivera about the office assistant job at (347) 555-4568.

Page 20, Exercise A

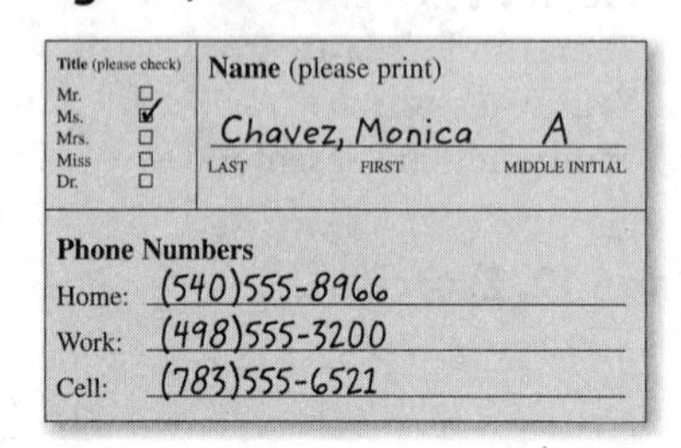

Title (please check): Mr. ☐ Ms. ☑ Mrs. ☐ Miss ☐ Dr. ☐

Name (please print): Chavez, Monica A
LAST FIRST MIDDLE INITIAL

Phone Numbers
Home: (540)555-8966
Work: (498)555-3200
Cell: (783)555-6521

Page 20, Exercise B

Answers will vary.

Page 21, Exercise A

1. A: Are / B: am
2. A: Is / B: isn't OR 's not
3. A: Is / B: isn't OR 's not
4. A: Are / B: aren't OR 're not
5. A: Are / B: 'm not

Page 21, Exercise B

1. A: Is Rob an electrician?
   B: Yes, he is.
2. A: Are Sarah and Ann artists?
   B: No, they aren't. OR No, they're not.
3. A: Is Mr. Ruiz a gardener?
   B: Yes, he is.
4. A: Are Carl and Miguel cooks?
   B: No, they aren't. OR No, they're not.
5. A: Is Jason an accountant?
   B: No, he isn't. OR No, he's not.
6. A: Are Bianca and Sam doctors?
   B: Yes, they are.

Page 22, Exercise C

1. cook
2. child-care worker
3. electrician
4. accountant
5. office assistant
6. accountant
7. artist
8. child-care worker
9. cook

Page 22, Exercise D

1. B: Is Rodrigo an electrician
   A: No, he isn't. He's an artist. OR No, he's not. He's an artist.
2. B: Is Ms. Torres a child-care worker
   A: Yes, she is.
3. B: Is Robert a cook
   A: Yes, he is.
4. B: Are Elena and Kristina office assistants
   A: No, they aren't. They're accountants. OR No, they're not. They're accountants.

Page 23, Exercise B

1. No, she isn't. OR No, she's not.
2. Yes, she is.
3. No, he isn't. OR No, he's not.
4. No, he isn't. OR No, he's not.
5. Yes, he is.
6. Yes, he is.

Page 23, Exercise C

Answers will vary.

Page 24, Exercise A

1. work / c
2. work / e
3. works / b
4. work / a
5. works / d

Page 24, Exercise B

1. work
2. works
3. work
4. work
5. works
6. works

Page 24, Exercise C

1. d   2. c   3. a   4. b

Page 25, Exercise D

1. are / live / works / work
2. is / works / lives
3. live / are / work

Page 25, Exercise E

Edna: Hi, I'm Edna.
Sam: Hi, Edna. I'm Sam.
Edna: It's nice to meet you.
Sam: It's nice to meet you, too.
Edna: Are you a student here?
Sam: No, I'm not. I'm a teacher.
Edna: Really? That's interesting.
Sam: What do you do, Edna?
Edna: I'm an artist.
Sam: Really? Where do you work?
Edna: I work in Boston.
Sam: That's great!

UNIT 3

Page 26, Exercise A

1. board
2. chalk
3. computer
4. desk
5. chair
6. book
7. cell phone
8. backpack

Page 27, Exercise B

1. piece of paper
2. eraser
3. CD
4. folder
5. three-ring binder
6. notebook
7. dictionary
8. marker

Page 27, Exercise C

1. on the desk
2. in the backpack
3. on the desk
4. in the backpack
5. on the desk

Page 28, Exercise A

1. Write
2. Listen
3. Turn off
4. Try to

Page 28, Exercise B

1. Don't look at the book.
2. Don't write your name.
3. Don't open your dictionary.
4. Don't take out your notebook.
5. Don't use a pencil.
6. Don't bring your book.

Page 29, Exercise C

1. Don't use a pen.
2. Don't take out your notebook.
3. Take out your book.
4. Look at the picture.
5. Use a pencil.
6. Don't eat in class.

Page 30, Exercise A

Student's Name: Paulo (FIRST) Brito (LAST) ☑M ☐F
Phone: (385)555-1497
Subject: English 2
Teacher: Mr. Franklin
Classroom: 312

Page 30, Exercise B

Answers will vary.

Page 31, Exercise B

1. True
2. True
3. False
4. False
5. False

Page 31, Exercise C

Answers will vary.

Page 32, Exercise A

1. This
2. These
3. Those
4. That

Page 32, Exercise B

1. Those are great backpacks.
2. These are good markers.
3. Those are my books.
4. These are great keyboards.
5. These are my binders.
6. Those are good dictionaries.

Page 32, Exercise C

1. That is / computer
2. Those are / chairs
3. This is / monitor
4. These are / books

Page 33, Exercise D

1. A: Is this a monitor?
   B: Yes, it is.
2. A: Is that a keyboard?
   B: No, it isn't. OR No, it's not.
3. A: Is this a binder?
   B: Yes, it is.
4. A: Are these folders?
   B: No, they aren't. OR No, they're not.
5. A: Is this a DVD?
   B: No, it isn't. OR No, it's not.
6. A: Are those CDs?
   B: Yes, they are.

Page 33, Exercise E

1. c   3. c   5. c   7. b
2. a   4. b   6. a

Page 34, Exercise A

1. 18   6. 62
2. 23   7. 74
3. 35   8. 89
4. 46   9. 97
5. 58   10. 100

Page 34, Exercise B

1. twenty-five
2. forty-two
3. fourteen
4. eighty-four
5. seventy-one
6. sixty
7. thirty-six
8. one hundred

Page 34, Exercise C

Directory

Cafeteria	17
Computer Lab	23
Library	28
Main Office	19

Page 35, Exercise D

1. the restroom
2. the cafeteria
3. Room 114
4. the computer lab
5. Room 216
6. Room 215

Page 35, Exercise E

1. It's across from Room 217.
2. It's next to Room 216.
3. It's across from the office.
4. It's next to Room 116.
5. It's across from the cafeteria.

Page 36, Exercise A

1. her
2. him
3. her
4. him
5. her

Page 36, Exercise C

1. Please call her.
2. Don't open it.
3. Please help them.
4. How do you spell it?
5. Call her about the job.
6. Ask him for help.

Page 37, Exercise D

1. me
2. him
3. them
4. her
5. us
6. them
7. it
8. them
9. you
10. us

Page 37, Exercise E

Bob: Excuse me. Can you help me?
Meg: Sure.
Bob: What room is the ESL office?
Meg: Sorry. I don't know. Ask him.
Bob: Uh . . . Who's he?
Meg: That's Mr. Smith, the custodian.
Bob: Excuse me. Which way is the ESL office?
Mr. Smith: It's down the hall on the left, Room 24.
Bob: Thank you.
Mr. Smith: You're welcome.

UNIT 4

Page 38, Exercise A

1. parents
2. daughter
3. children
4. wife
5. son
6. grandmother
7. husband
8. sister
9. mother
10. brother
11. grandfather
12. father

Page 38, Exercise B

Male	Female	Male and Female
father	mother	parents
son	daughter	children
grandfather	grandmother	
brother	sister	
husband	wife	

Page 39, Exercise C

1. They're Robert's parents.
2. He's Robert's father.
3. She's Robert's mother.
4. She's Robert's wife.
5. They're Robert's children.
6. He's Robert's son.
7. She's Robert's daughter.

Page 39, Exercise D

1. He's / brother
2. He's / grandfather
3. She's / grandmother
4. She's / sister

Page 40, Exercise A

1. My
2. Your
3. His
4. Her
5. Their
6. our

Page 40, Exercise B

1. her
2. Their
3. her / their
4. our
5. his / their
6. Our

Page 40, Exercise C

1. my
2. their
3. her
4. his
5. his
6. his

Page 41, Exercise D

1. Jack's
2. Stanley's
3. Monique's
4. Molly's
5. Monique's

Page 41, Exercise E

Eva: That's a great photo. Who's that?
Tom: That's my sister, Fran.
Eva: She looks nice. Is that your mother?
Tom: Yes, it is.
Eva: Fran looks like her.
Tom: Yes. And this is my brother, Tim.
Eva: He looks like your mother, too.
Tom: I know. And I look like my father.

Page 42, Exercise B

1. a 3. b 5. a 7. a
2. b 4. b 6. a 8. a

Page 42, Exercise C

Answers will vary.

Page 43, Exercise A

1. has
2. is
3. are
4. am / have
5. is / has
6. is / has
7. are / have

Page 43, Exercise B

1. 's / has
2. has / 's
3. 's / has
4. 's / has
5. 's / has

Page 43, Exercise C

4, 5, 2, 1, 3

Page 44, Exercise D

1. Philip is short and average weight. He has short hair.
2. Alex is tall and thin. He has a mustache and a beard. He has short hair.
3. Ivan is average height and heavy. He has long hair.

Page 44, Exercise E

Mary: *Is your family here in this country?*
Luz: Well, my brother and sister are here. My parents are in Mexico.
Mary: *What's your brother like?*
Luz: He's great.
Mary: *Does he look like you?*
Luz: Yes. He's tall and thin and has short hair.
Mary: What about your sister? *Does she look like you?*
Luz: No. She's average height and heavy. She has long hair.

Page 45, Exercise A

FEBRUARY

Sunday	Monday	Tuesday	Wednesday	Thursday	Friday	Saturday
1	2	3	4	(5) Judy's birthday	6	7
8	(9) Randy's birthday	10	11	12	13	14
(15) Kevin's birthday	16	17	18	(19) Martha's birthday	20	21
22	23	(24) James's birthday	25	26	27	28

Page 45, Exercise B

1. Judy's birthday is February 5.
2. Randy's birthday is February 9.
3. Kevin's birthday is February 15.
4. Martha's birthday is February 19.
5. James's birthday is February 24.

Page 46, Exercise C

1. March 18, 1975
2. August 30, 1945
3. November 29, 1985
4. February 17, 1969
5. May 22, 1981
6. December 21, 1984

Page 46, Exercise D

1. 5-4-04
2. 10-8-83
3. 1-7-99
4. 9-26-03
5. 7-28-52
6. 5-13-95
7. 3-12-07
8. 4-9-74

Page 47, Exercise A

1. A: is
   B: He's
2. A: are
   B: is / is
3. A: is
   B: He's
4. A: are
   B: They're
5. A: is
   B: she's

Page 47, Exercise B

Holt Central School District

Parents
Father: *Hernandez, Martin* Mother: *Hernandez, Anna*

Children	Age	Grade
José	14	9
Carmen	11	6
Miguel	8	3

Page 48, Exercise D

1. How old is / He's / years old
2. Is he in / he isn't OR he's not. He's in the fifth grade.
3. How old is / She's / years old
4. Is she in / she is
5. How old is / He's / years old
6. Is he in / he isn't OR he's not. He's in the ninth grade.

Page 48, Exercise E

Mark: Hi, Nina. Where are you?
Nina: *I'm at my cousin's house.* I'm babysitting for her kids.
Mark: Oh, that's nice. *How old are they?*
Nina: Well, her daughter is nine. *She's in the fourth grade. And her son is seven.* He's in the second grade.

Page 49, Exercise A

Emergency Contact Information

Name: *Escovar* (last), *Sandra* (first)

In case of emergency, call:

Name	Relationship	Daytime Phone	Evening Phone	Other Phone
Carlos Escovar	Husband	(498)555-2221	(498)555-2379	(495)555-3696
Monica Ortiz	Mother	(674)555-9876	—	—

Page 49, Exercise B

Answers will vary.

UNIT 5

Page 50, Exercise A

1. a dress, shoes
2. a sweater, pants, socks
3. a jacket, jeans, sneakers
4. a T-shirt, jeans, socks
5. a shirt, pants, shoes
6. a blouse, a skirt, shoes

Page 51, Exercise B

Singular	Plural
a dress	socks
a shirt	sneakers
a blouse	jeans
a sweater	pants
a skirt	shoes
a jacket	
a T-shirt	

Page 51, Exercise C

1. It's a yellow shirt.
2. They're black socks.
3. It's a pink dress.
4. They're red sneakers.
5. It's a purple jacket.
6. They're beige pants.

Page 51, Exercise D

1. yellow / green
2. red
3. red

Page 51, Exercise E

Answers will vary.

Page 52, Exercise A

1. needs
2. needs
3. need
4. need
5. need
6. needs
7. need
8. need

Page 52, Exercise B

1. Carla has a new watch.
2. Alex and Sufia have black pants.
3. I have new shoes.
4. Matthew has a new sweater and jeans.
5. We have new blouses.
6. Eric has a yellow backpack.
7. Luis and Mark have new sneakers.
8. You have a brown jacket.
9. We have new shirts.
10. Mr. Lee has black shoes.

Page 53, Exercise C

1. Ricardo wants a new backpack and sneakers.
2. Sarah and Tina want new blouses and skirts.
3. Carl wants a new jacket and pants.
4. Thomas and Sam want new T-shirts and watches.

Page 53, Exercise D

1. wants
2. needs
3. has
4. want
5. need
6. have
7. needs
8. have
9. want
10. has

Page 53, Exercise E

Answers will vary.

Page 54, Exercise A

1. c 2. a 3. d 4. b

Page 54, Exercise B

1. 5¢ 2. 1¢ 3. 25¢ 4. 10¢

Page 54, Exercise C

1. $5.00
2. $20.00
3. $10.00
4. $1.00

Page 54, Exercise D

1. 52¢
2. 55¢
3. $1.86
4. $32.14

Page 55, Exercise E

1. 5¢
2. $10.01
3. $6.00
4. $3.00
5. $2.00

Page 55, Exercise F

1. b 3. b 5. b
2. a 4. b 6. b

Page 56, Exercise A

1. Joe's Jeans
2. September 15, 2009
3. $29.95
4. $39.95
5. $12.95
6. $5.80
7. $82.85
8. $88.65
9. $1.35

Page 56, Exercise B

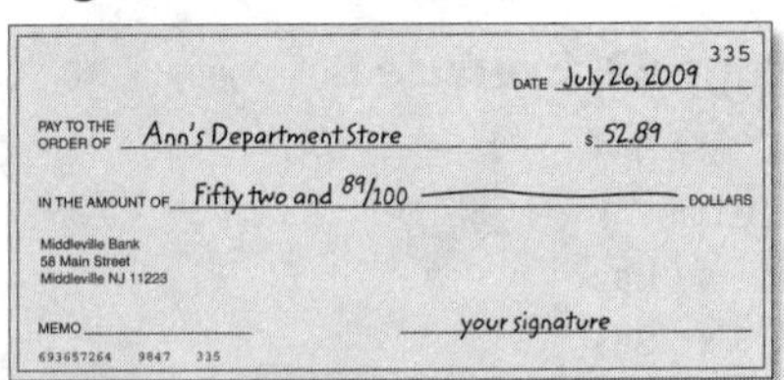

Page 57, Exercise A

1. A: Do
   B: do
2. A: Does
   B: doesn't
3. A: Do
   B: don't
4. A: Does
   B: does
5. A: Do
   B: do
6. A: Do
   B: don't

Page 57, Exercise B

1. Do you have this sweater in a large?
2. Does she want this T-shirt in a medium?
3. Does Tom have a black jacket?
4. Do you like these shoes?
5. Do you have this skirt in blue?
6. Do you have this dress in a medium?

Page 58, Exercise C

1. A: Do / have
   B: do
2. A: Does / need
   B: doesn't / has
3. A: Do / like
   B: do
4. A: Do / need
   B: don't / have
5. A: Does / want
   B: does / likes
6. A: Do / have
   B: don't / have

Page 58, Exercise D

1. Yes, she does.
2. Yes, she does.
3. No, she doesn't.
4. Yes, she does.
5. No, she doesn't.
6. Yes, they do.
7. No, she doesn't.

Page 59, Exercise B

1. True
2. False
3. True
4. False
5. True
6. True

Page 59, Exercise C

Answers will vary.

Page 60, Exercise A

1. don't
2. doesn't
3. don't
4. doesn't
5. don't
6. doesn't

Page 60, Exercise B

1. don't need
2. don't like
3. doesn't like
4. doesn't fit
5. don't want
6. doesn't need

Page 61, Exercise C

1. He doesn't like the red jacket.
2. She doesn't want the orange sneakers.
3. They don't need new jeans.
4. I don't have my receipt.
5. These pants don't fit.
6. This jacket doesn't fit.
7. She doesn't have a brown backpack.

Page 61, Exercise D

1. The shirt doesn't fit.
2. The watch doesn't work.
3. She doesn't like the jacket.
4. The dress doesn't fit.

UNIT 6

Page 62, Exercise A

1. sofa
2. closet
3. sink
4. bed
5. shower

Page 62, Exercise B

1. microwave
2. refrigerator
3. sink
4. lamp
5. toilet
6. bed

Page 63, Exercise C

1. lamp / bedroom
2. dresser / bedroom
3. stove / kitchen
4. chair / dining room
5. table / living room

Page 64, Exercise A

1. In my house, *there's* a living room, and *there's* a small kitchen, but *there's* no dining room. *There are* two bedrooms, but *there's* no laundry room. *There's* one bathroom. *There's* a garage. *There are* no closets.
2. In my house, *there's* a large living room, and *there's* a large kitchen, too. *There's* a small dining room. *There are* two bathrooms and three bedrooms. *There are* two closets, also. *There's* a laundry room, but *there's* no garage.
3. In my house, *there's* a living room, but *there's* no dining room. *There's* one bedroom. *There's* one bathroom, but *there are* no closets. *There's* a kitchen, and *there's* a garage.

Page 64, Exercise B

Paragraph 1: Floor Plan C
Paragraph 2: Floor Plan B
Paragraph 3: Floor Plan A

Page 65, Exercise C

1. b 2. a 3. a 4. a

Page 65, Exercise D

1. There's a sofa. There's a table, and there's a chair. There are no lamps.
2. There's a sofa. There are two lamps. There's no chair and there's no table.

Page 66, Exercise B

1. large
2. living room
3. kitchen
4. small
5. two
6. five
7. a garage

Page 66, Exercise C

Answers will vary.

Page 67, Exercise A

1. Is there / Yes, there is.
2. Is there / No, there isn't. OR No, there's not.
3. Is there / Yes, there is.
4. Is there / Yes, there is.
5. Are there / Yes, there are.
6. Are there / No, there aren't.
7. Is there / No, there isn't. OR No, there's not.
8. Is there / No, there isn't. OR No, there's not.
9. Is there / Yes, there is.
10. Are there / No, there aren't.

Page 68, Exercise B

1. A: Is there a studio apartment for rent?
   B: Yes, there is. There's an unfurnished apartment for rent.
   A: Is there a refrigerator?
   B: Yes, there is. There's a new refrigerator.
   A: Are there closets?
   B: No, there are no closets.
   A: Is there a stove?
   B: No, there's no stove.
2. A: Is there a one-bedroom apartment for rent?
   B: Yes, there is. There's a furnished apartment for rent.
   A: Are there appliances?
   B: Yes, there are. There are new appliances.
   A: Is there a bed?
   B: Yes, there is. There's a new bed.
   A: Is there a dining room?
   B: No, there's no dining room.
3. A: Is there a two-bedroom apartment for rent?
   B: Yes, there is. There's an unfurnished apartment for rent.
   A: Is there a microwave?
   B: Yes, there is. There's a microwave.
   A: Are there closets?
   B: Yes, there are. There are four closets.
   A: Is there a laundry room?
   B: No, there's no laundry room.

Page 69, Exercise A

1. b 2. a 3. b 4. a 5. a

Page 69, Exercise B

1. St.
2. Dr.
3. Ave.
4. Blvd.
5. Rd.

Page 69, Exercise C

Possible sentences:

There's a two-bedroom apartment for rent.
There's a large kitchen.
There's a dining room.
There's air conditioning.
There's parking.
Utilities are included.
The rent is $1,800 a month.

Page 70, Exercise D

1. c 2. e 3. a 4. b 5. d

Page 70, Exercise E

1.

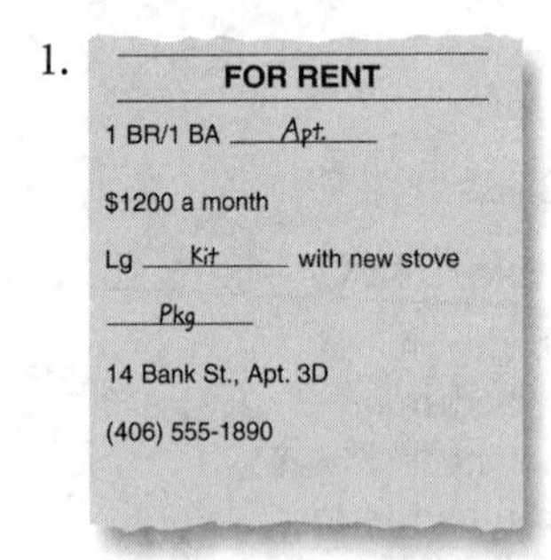

FOR RENT
1 BR/1 BA Apt.
$1200 a month
Lg Kit with new stove
Pkg
14 Bank St., Apt. 3D
(406) 555-1890

2.

FOR RENT
2 BR/1 BA Apt.
$1300 a month
Lg BA with new shower
Utils. incl.
346 Clover Blvd., Apt. 1C
(317) 555-1299

3.

FOR RENT
3 BR/2 BA in new bldg.
$1450 a month
Lg DR
45 Orchard Ave., Apt. 2B
(836) 555-6978

4.

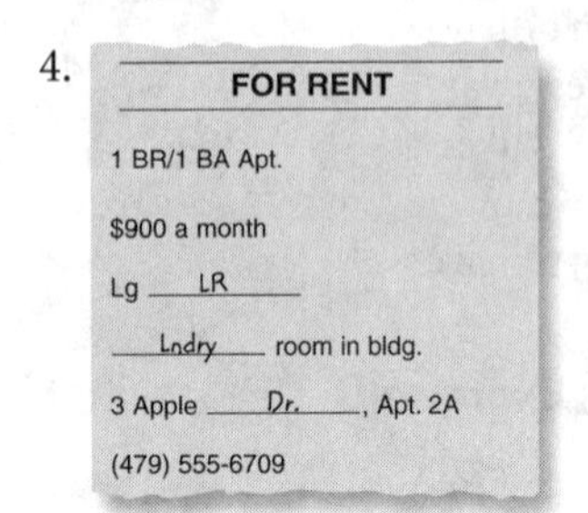

FOR RENT
1 BR/1 BA Apt.
$900 a month
Lg LR
Lndry room in bldg.
3 Apple Dr., Apt. 2A
(479) 555-6709

Page 71, Exercise A

Page 71, Exercise B

Answers will vary.

Page 72, Exercise A

1. from
2. at
3. in
4. to
5. on
6. at

Page 72, Exercise B

A: How do I get to Century Department Store?

B: From here? Let's see. Go east on Maple Avenue. Turn left at Bank Street. Then continue on Bank Street to 6th Street. It's on the corner of Bank and 6th.

Page 72, Exercise C

Sam: Hi, Jess. Are you coming **to** my house?

Jess: Yes, Sam. How do I get there **from** here? I'm coming **from** my office.

Sam: My apartment is **in** Oakdale. First, go **to** Conner Street. Turn left. Continue north **on** Conner Street. Then turn left **at** the light. That's Manor Road. My house is **at** 58 Manor Road.

Jess: Great!

Page 73, Exercise D

Go (south / **north**) (in /**on**) Powell Street. Continue (at / **on**) Powell Street for three blocks. Turn right (on/ **at**) the (3rd / **2nd**) light. Continue (**east** / west) (in / **on**) Starrett Street. Our store is (at / **on**) Starrett Street (in / **on**) the (left / **right**). It's (**at** / in) 3228 Starrett Street.

Page 73, Exercise E

Ed's Appliances

Page 73, Exercise F

Go **south** **on** Powell Street. Continue **on** Powell Street for one block. Turn left **at** the light. Continue **on** Starrett Street for two blocks. Go **right** on Reed Avenue. Continue **on** Reed Avenue for two blocks. Turn **left** on Oak Street. It's **at** 4118 Oak Street.

UNIT 7

Page 74, Exercise A

1. the dishes
2. breakfast
3. to work
4. a shower
5. dressed

Page 74, Exercise B

1. gets home
2. exercises
3. cooks dinner
4. eats dinner
5. washes the dishes / watches TV
6. reads the newspaper
7. takes a shower
8. goes to sleep

Page 75, Exercise C

1. A: get up
   B: 5:00
2. A: take a shower
   B: 5:15
3. A: get dressed
   B: 5:30
4. A: eat breakfast
   B: 5:45
5. A: go to work
   B: 6:00

Page 75, Exercise D

Answers will vary.

Page 76, Exercise A

1. do / work
2. does / get up
3. do / have
4. do / go
5. does / start
6. does / get

Page 76, Exercise B

1. A: What time do you get home?
   B: At 6:30.
2. A: What time do they go to work?
   B: At 7:15.
3. A: What time does Arnold exercise?
   B: At 12:00.
4. A: What time does she eat breakfast?
   B: At 6:00.
5. A: What time do Jason and Marie eat dinner?
   B: At 5:30.

Page 77, Exercise C

1. From / to / on
2. On
3. From / to
4. At
5. At / on

Page 77, Exercise D

1. She works on Sundays from 12:00 to 5:00.
2. She has English class on Wednesdays from 7:00 to 9:00.
3. She plays soccer on Thursdays from 4:00 to 7:00.
4. She babysits on Fridays from 3:00 to 6:00.
5. She has a computer class on Saturdays from 1:00 to 3:00.

Page 78, Exercise A

Sunday	Monday	Tuesday	Wednesday	Thursday	Friday	Saturday
		10:00–2:00 work	1:00-5:00 English class	10:00–2:00 work		

Page 78, Exercise B

1. 7:00 P.M. / 12:00 A.M. / Tuesdays / Thursdays
2. Mondays / Wednesdays / Fridays
3. 9:00 A.M.
4. 1:00 P.M.
5. 6:00 A.M. / 12:00 P.M.
6. 20

Page 79, Exercise C

1. Tuesdays / Thursdays / Saturdays
2. 11:00 A.M.
3. 11:00 A.M / 7:00 P.M.
4. 8:00 A.M.
5. Saturdays

Page 79, Exercise D

Answers will vary.

Page 80, Exercise A

TIME SHEET			
EMPLOYEE NAME		EMPLOYEE I.D. #	
Last: Vlahos	First: Elisa	459876	
		Week ending 11/14	
DAY	TIME IN	TIME OUT	HOURS
Mon.	4:00 P.M.	11:00 P.M.	7
Tues.	4:00 P.M.	11:00 P.M.	7
Wed.	4:00 P.M.	11:00 P.M.	7
Thurs.	4:00 P.M.	11:00 P.M.	7
Fri.			
Sat.			
Sun.	4:00 P.M.	11:00 P.M.	7
Employee Signature: Elisa Vlahos		TOTAL HOURS: 35	

Page 80, Exercise B

Answers will vary.

Page 81, Exercise A

1. always
2. always
3. always
4. usually
5. sometimes
6. never

Page 81, Exercise B

1. Sarah usually shops for food on Saturdays.
2. Martin always takes a shower at night.
3. Conor sometimes rides his bike on Sundays.
4. They never do the laundry on Sundays.

Page 82, Exercise C

1. He usually goes to the park.
2. She sometimes plays basketball.
3. He always shops for food.
4. He never goes dancing.
5. She sometimes cleans. OR She sometimes cleans the kitchen. OR She sometimes cleans the house.
6. She always goes swimming.

Page 82, Exercise D

Answers will vary.

Page 83, Exercise B

1. Irma works ~~in the mornings~~ [at night].
2. She works ~~two~~ [three] nights a week.
3. Her husband works ~~at night~~ [days].
4. ~~She~~ [Her husband] works on Saturdays.
5. ~~Her husband~~ [She OR Irma] shops for food.
6. On ~~Saturdays~~ [Sundays], Irma and her husband take the children to the park or zoo.

Page 83, Exercise C

Answers will vary.

Page 84, Exercise A

1. He goes running every day.
2. He studies English twice a week.
3. He works on his car twice a week.
4. He plays basketball once a week.
5. He works five days a week.
6. He has class four times a week.
7. He shops for food once a week.
8. He sees a movie once a week.

Page 85, Exercise B

Go running: Three times a week
Take a long walk: Once a week
Do puzzles: Every day
Listen to music: Never

Page 85, Exercise C

1. does / listen to music
2. do / go running
3. do / play video games
4. does / ride her bike
5. does / work
6. do / have English class

Page 85, Exercise D

Answers will vary.

UNIT 8

Page 86, Exercise A

1. yogurt
2. cereal
3. oranges
4. apples
5. bananas
6. eggs
7. bread
8. butter

Page 86, Exercise B

1. cabbage
2. onions
3. chicken
4. potatoes
5. rice
6. beans
7. milk
8. beef
9. lettuce
10. cheese

Page 87, Exercise C

1. grains
2. vegetables
3. fruit
4. meat / beans
5. dairy

Page 87, Exercise D

Answers will vary.

Page 87, Exercise E

Answers will vary.

Page 88, Exercise A

Count	Non-count
apple	beef
cookie	butter
egg	cake
pancake	cereal
potato	lettuce
taco	yogurt

Page 88, Exercise B

1. bananas / them
2. steak / it
3. yogurt / it
4. cereal / it
5. potatoes / them
6. eggs / them

Page 89, Exercise C

1. pancakes
2. apples
3. oranges
4. cabbage
5. apple pie
6. pasta

Page 89, Exercise D

1. A: a hamburger
2. A: a taco / tacos
   B: a taco
3. A: pizza
   B: Pizza / pizza
   A: pizza
4. A: cake / cake

Page 90, Exercise A

Shopping List

milk
orange juice
4 tomatoes
3 onions
steak
cheese
bread
cereal
pasta

Page 90, Exercise B

Answers will vary.

Page 91, Exercise B

1. True
2. False
3. False
4. True
5. True
6. False

Page 91, Exercise C

Answers will vary.

Page 92, Exercise A

1. Do you want iced tea or coffee?
2. Do you want fries or salad?
3. Do you want pizza or a sandwich?
4. Do you want fries or a baked potato?
5. Do you want milk or juice?
6. Do you want steak or a hamburger?

Page 92, Exercise B

1. Would you like soup or salad?
2. Would you like bread or rice?
3. Would you like fries or a baked potato?
4. Would you like chicken or fish?
5. Would you like cake or ice cream?

Page 93, Exercise C

1. a
2. b
3. b
4. b
5. b
6. a

Page 93, Exercise D

Date

Burger Heaven
Guest Check

a green salad	
a hamburger	
large fries	
a large soda	
a bowl of soup	
a chicken sandwich	
a baked potato	
a large iced tea	
apple pie	

Page 94, Exercise A

1. $4.29 a pound
2. 99¢ a pound
3. $4.29
4. $3.29 a pound
5. $6.99 a pound
6. 79¢ a pound
7. 89¢

Page 94, Exercise B

Page 95, Exercise C

1. b 2. a 3. b 4. b 5. a

Page 95, Exercise D

1. 10
2. 9
3. 120
4. 110
5. 150 milligrams
6. 220 milligrams
7. 12 grams
8. 24 grams
9. Cereal B

Page 96, Exercise A

1. A: How much butter
   B: Not much
2. A: How many onions
   B: Not many
3. A: How much ice cream
   B: A lot
4. A: How much milk
   B: Not much
5. A: How much yogurt
   B: A lot
6. A: How much cereal
   B: A lot
7. A: How many tomatoes
   B: Not many
8. A: How many peppers
   B: A lot

Page 97, Exercise B

1. A: How much turkey
   B: two pounds
2. A: How much rice
   B: twelve ounces
3. A: How many peppers
   B: two
4. A: How many onions
   B: three
5. A: How much milk
   B: eight ounces
6. A: How much cheese
   B: ten ounces
7. A: How much vegetable oil
   B: two ounces

Page 97, Exercise C

Check (✓) the following foods:
apple pie; green salad; grilled chicken; juice; rice; soda; water

UNIT 9

Page 98, Exercise A

hot: 95–110
warm: 70–85
cool: 45–60
cold: 20–35

Page 98, Exercise B

1. c 2. d 3. a 4. b

Page 99, Exercise C

1. It's warm and cloudy.
2. It's cool and rainy.
3. It's hot and sunny.
4. It's cold and snowy.

Page 99, Exercise D

Answers will vary.

Page 100, Exercise A

1. is not working
2. are visiting
3. is not sleeping
4. is studying
5. are not eating
6. are making

Page 100, Exercise B

1. She's talking on the phone.
2. We're watching TV.
3. I'm reading a book.
4. It's raining in Chicago.
5. He's riding his bike.
6. They're running in the park.
7. She's wearing a new jacket.
8. We're visiting our friends in Miami.

Page 101, Exercise C

1. 's talking
2. isn't drinking OR 's not drinking
3. isn't eating OR 's not eating
4. isn't doing OR 's not doing
5. 's listening
6. 's doing
7. 's drinking
8. isn't talking OR 's not talking
9. 're sitting
10. aren't watching TV OR 're not watching TV

Page 101, Exercise D

1. He's cleaning.
2. She's listening to music.
3. She's sleeping.
4. He's reading.
5. She's cooking.

Page 102

Sample postcard:

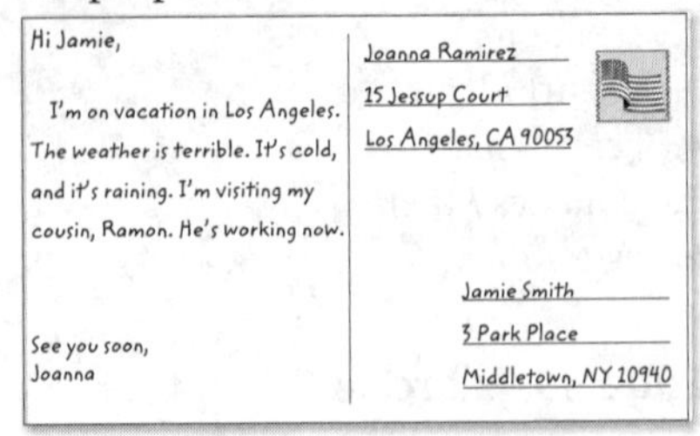

Page 103, Exercise A

1. d 3. f 5. c
2. b 4. e 6. a

Page 103, Exercise B

Circle the following items:
flashlight; bottle of water; matches; candles; batteries

Page 104, Exercise C

Sample answers:
1. Buy batteries and a flashlight.
2. Stay in the house.
3. Leave your house.

Page 104, Exercise D

Answers will vary.

Page 104, Exercise E

Answers will vary.

Page 105, Exercise A

1. a. No, she isn't. OR No, she's not.
   b. Yes, she is.
   c. Yes, she is.
2. a. Yes, he is.
   b. No, he isn't. OR No, he's not.
   c. Yes, he is.
3. a. No, it isn't. OR No, it's not.
   b. No, they aren't. OR No, they're not.
   c. Yes, they are.

Page 106, Exercise B

1. A: Is / studying English
   B: she isn't OR she's not
2. A: Are / listening to music?
   B: I'm not
3. A: Are / shopping for food
   B: I'm not
4. A: Is / raining
   B: it is
5. A: Are / going home
   B: they aren't OR they're not
6. A: Is / snowing
   B: it isn't OR it's not

Page 106, Exercise C

Ann: Are you watching the news?
Tim: *No, I'm not. I'm reading a magazine.*
Ann: Well, turn on the TV. A big storm is coming.
Tim: *Really?*
Ann: Yes. In fact, I'm coming home early. I'm at the grocery store now.
Tim: *Oh, good. Are you getting water?*
Ann: Yes. I'm getting water, food, and a lot of batteries.
Tim: *Great. Get matches, too.*
Ann: OK. Do we need anything else?
Tim: *Yes. We need good weather!*

Page 107, Exercise B

1. Mike
2. Mike's mother
3. Mike's mother
4. Mike
5. Mike's mother
6. Mike

Page 107, Exercise C

Answers will vary.

Page 108, Exercise A

1. earmuffs / gloves
2. sunblock
3. a raincoat / an umbrella
4. sunglasses
5. a scarf / boots

Page 108, Exercise B

1. It's really hot and humid in Dallas today.
2. It's pretty cold and snowing in Boston now. OR It's snowing and pretty cold in Boston now.
3. It's very foggy in San Francisco in the winter.
4. The weather in New York is pretty nice in the spring.

Page 109, Exercise C

1. b 2. a 3. b 4. a 5. b

UNIT 10

Page 110, Exercise A

1. a supermarket
2. a department store
3. an ATM
4. a bank
5. a park
6. a drugstore
7. a laundromat
8. a coffee shop
9. a gas station
10. a fire station
11. a post office
12. a bus stop
13. a police station
14. a parking lot
15. a hair salon

Page 111, Exercise B

1. on Seaview Boulevard
2. on Oyster Road
3. on Seaview Boulevard
4. on Oyster Road
5. on Erie Street
6. on Oyster Road
7. on Seaview Boulevard
8. on Seaview Boulevard OR on Erie Street

Page 111, Exercise C

1. c 3. a 5. d
2. e 4. f 6. b

Page 112, Exercise A

1. on / between
2. on / next to
3. next to
4. across from
5. on the corner of
6. down
7. next to
8. around the corner

Page 113, Exercise B

1. on the corner of
2. near
3. between
4. down the block
5. near
6. on the corner of
7. around the corner
8. down the block
9. around the corner
10. between

Page 113, Exercise C

1. the coffee shop
2. the nursing home
3. the supermarket

Page 114, Exercise A

1. I drive.
2. She rides her bike.
3. They take the subway.
4. She takes the bus.
5. He takes a taxi.
6. They take the train.

Page 115, Exercise B

1. c 2. e 3. b 4. d 5. a

Page 115, Exercise C

1. 8:40
2. Maple Avenue
3. 8:52
4. 8:44
5. 4th Avenue
6. 8:53
7. 9:06
8. South Drive
9. Elm Street
10. 9:08

Page 116, Exercise A

Meg: How do you get to the high school?
Rob: Take the Number 12 train.
Meg: Ok. Where do you get the train?
Rob: Around the corner on Colombo Road.
Meg: Great. Where do you buy a ticket?
Rob: In the station.
Meg: Thanks. One more question. How much does the train cost?
Rob: $2.50.

Page 116, Exercise C

Mark: Which bus goes to the high school?
Lisa: The Number 27 bus goes to the high school.
Mark: OK. What time does the bus leave the station?
Lisa: At 7:15.
Mark: How much does the bus cost?
Lisa: $3.50.
Mark: Thanks. One more question. Where do you get off?
Lisa: Dupont Square.

Page 117, Exercise E

A: How do you get to Watertown High School?
B: Take the Number 8 bus.
A: Where do you get it?
B: At Crawford Street.
A: How much does it cost?
B: $3.50.
A: Where do you get off?
B: At Newport Avenue.

Page 117, Exercise F

1. How do you get to Nick's Coffee Shop?
2. How much does the train cost?
3. Where do you get off?
4. Where do you get the Number 6 bus?
5. How much does the bus cost?
6. How do you get to the library?
7. Where do you buy a ticket for the bus?
8. How do you get to the train station?

Page 118

Sample answers:

1. Walk down Dogwood Lane. Turn left on Bond Boulevard. The drugstore is on the corner of Oak Street and Bond Boulevard.
2. Walk down Dogwood Lane. Turn left on Seaman Drive. Continue on Seaman Drive for three blocks. The supermarket is on the right.

Page 119, Exercise B

1. Omar works at Watertown ~~Post Office~~ Hospital.
2. He drives to work on ~~Mondays~~ Sundays.
3. From Monday to Thursday he takes the ~~train~~ bus.
4. He gets the ~~train~~ bus down the block from his house.
5. He gets off the bus at ~~State~~ Sutton Street.
6. The hospital is ~~down the block~~ around the corner form the bus station.

Page 119, Exercise C

Answers will vary.

Page 120, Exercise A

A: are / doing
B: 'm going
A: are / going
B: 's going
A: are / getting
B: 're driving

Page 120, Exercise B

1. A: is
   B: He's going to a concert
2. A: are
   B: I'm playing basketball
3. A: are
   B: They're going to the mall. OR They're going shopping.
4. A: 's
   B: She's riding her bike.
5. A: 's
   B: He's studying.

Page 121, Exercise C

1. Where is he going this weekend?
2. What are you doing on Saturday night?
3. Who are you going with to the movies?
4. How is your sister getting to the concert?
5. Who are you playing soccer with on Sunday?
6. What are they doing on Friday night?

Page 121, Exercise D

UNIT 11

Page 122, Exercise A

1. head
2. face
3. eye
4. teeth
5. mouth
6. ear
7. nose
8. hand
9. elbow
10. chest
11. shoulder
12. stomach
13. leg
14. foot
15. wrist
16. arm
17. neck
18. back
19. knee
20. ankle

Page 123, Exercise B

Parts of the head	Parts of the arm	Parts of the leg
ears	elbow	ankle
eyes	hand	foot
mouth	wrist	knee
nose		

Page 123, Exercise C

1. feet
2. leg
3. head
4. hands
5. shoulders
6. arms

Page 124, Exercise A

A: do / feel
B: feel
A: Do / have
B: don't have / hurts

Page 124, Exercise B

1. the flu
2. a headache
3. a stomachache
4. an earache

Page 125, Exercise C

1. has / doesn't have
2. don't feel / have
3. has / hurts
4. doesn't feel / hurts
5. feels / has
6. don't feel / have

Page 125, Exercise D

1. How does Erica feel?
2. Her head hurts.
3. Does she have a fever?
4. No, she doesn't have a fever.
5. Does she have a stuffy nose?
6. Yes, she has a stuffy nose.

Page 126, Exercise A

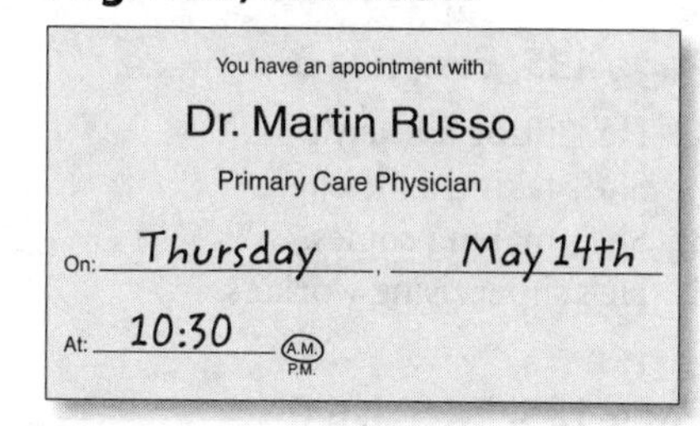

You have an appointment with
Dr. Martin Russo
Primary Care Physician
On: Thursday, May 14th
At: 10:30 A.M. P.M.

Page 126, Exercise B

Assistant: Children's Clinic. Can I help you?
Mrs. Pietro: This is Mrs. Pietro. I'd like to make an appointment for my son.
Assistant: Sure. What is your son's name?
Mrs. Pietro: His name is Alex.
Assistant: Can he come in on Thursday?
Mrs. Pietro: No, I'm sorry.
Assistant: How about Friday?
Mrs. Pietro: Yes, that's good.
Assistant: Is 4:30 OK?
Mrs. Pietro: Yes, we can be there.
Assistant: OK, that's Friday, January 31 at 4:30 P.M. See you then.

Page 127, Exercise C

1. step
2. sit
3. roll up
4. Open / say
5. take
6. lie down

Page 127, Exercise D

1. 6 hours / 2 tablets / No, he can't.
2. 4 hours / 1 tablet / Yes, she can.

Page 128

Answers will vary.

Page 129, Exercise A

1. was / wasn't
2. wasn't / was
3. wasn't /was
4. were / weren't
5. weren't / were

Page 129, Exercise B

1. is / was
2. are / were
3. are / were
4. is / was
5. is / was

Page 129, Exercise C

1. Kamila wasn't sick last night.
2. Lisa and Meg weren't in Peru last week.
3. We weren't in Japan last summer.
4. They weren't in the hospital yesterday.
5. My father wasn't sick yesterday morning.

Page 130, Exercise D

1. wasn't / was
2. was / wasn't
3. was / wasn't
4. was / was
5. was / wasn't
6. was
7. was

Page 130, Exercise E

I was in New York last night. I was at a party. It was a surprise party for my parents. The problem was that my parents weren't there. They were both at home. My parents were both sick. The surprise was on us! It wasn't much fun without my parents.

Page 131, Exercise B

1. doesn't go
2. drinks
3. goes
4. goes
5. often
6. was

Page 131, Exercise C

Answers will vary.

Page 132, Exercise A

1. should
2. shouldn't
3. should
4. shouldn't
5. should
6. shouldn't

Page 132, Exercise B

Sara: Hi, Joe. This is Sara.
Joe: Hi, Sara. How are you? Is something wrong?
Sara: Well, I'm sick. I'm not coming to work today.
Joe: Oh, I'm sorry to hear that. What do you have?
Sara: I'm not sure. I have a headache, and my stomach doesn't feel good.
Joe: Do you have a fever?
Sara: Yes, I do. I just feel terrible.
Joe: Well, take it easy, Sara. You should rest and drink a lot.
Sara: That's a good idea.
Joe: But call the doctor if you don't feel better soon. You really shouldn't wait too long.
Sara: OK. Thanks Joe.

Page 133, Exercise D

1. should use a heating pad
2. should take a hot shower
3. shouldn't take antibiotics
4. should eat a piece of onion
5. shouldn't put butter on it
6. shouldn't drink milk or juice

UNIT 12

Page 134, Exercise A

1. answers the phone
2. drives a truck
3. helps people
4. takes care of grounds
5. uses a computer
6. delivers packages

Page 135, Exercise B

1. He's lifting a heavy box.
2. She's taking a message.
3. She's making copies.
4. He's supervising workers.

Page 135, Exercise C

1. a computer
2. a message
3. rooms
4. offices
5. food
6. messages

Page 136, Exercise A

1. can organize
2. can use
3. can take
4. can write
5. can work
6. can make
7. can help
8. can speak

Page 136, Exercise B

1. can't
2. can
3. can't
4. can't
5. can
6. can
7. can
8. can't

Page 137, Exercise C

1. He can clean floors.
2. He can't take care of grounds.
3. He can't use a computer.
4. She can take messages.
5. He can fix things. OR He can fix sinks.
6. She can drive a truck.

Page 137, Exercise D

Answers will vary.

Page 138, Exercise A

Job Ad A

Page 138, Exercise B

1. part-time
2. $12
3. full-time
4. Job B
5. Job A
6. Job C

Page 138, Exercise C

1. Job B 2. Job C 3. Job A

Page 139, Exercise D

1. Job B
2. $340
3. Job B
4. Job C
5. Job A
6. Job A
7. $160

Page 139, Exercise E

Answers will vary.

Page 140, Exercise A

1. No, they can't.
2. Yes, she can.
3. Yes, they can.
4. Yes, she can.
5. No, he can't.
6. No, he can't.

Page 141, Exercise B

1. A: Can you work on Sunday mornings?
   B: Yes, I can.
2. A: Can you work on Monday nights?
   B: Yes, I can.
3. A: Can you work on Tuesday nights?
   B: No, I can't.
4. A: Can you work on Wednesday nights?
   B: Yes, I can.
5. A: Can you work on Friday nights?
   B: No, I can't.

Page 141, Exercise C

Mia: I'm here about a job. I noticed the help wanted sign.
Yao: OK. Which job?
Mia: The cashier's job. I can use a cash register.
Yao: Can you use a computer?
Mia: No, I can't, but I can learn.
Yao: Can you answer the phone?
Mia: Sure. I can answer the phone.
Yao: Can you start now?
Mia: Yes, I can.
Yao: Great! You can have the job! Welcome to Yao's Chinese Restaurant.

Page 142, Exercise B

Christine
Check (✓):
- Use a computer
- Fix computers
- Help people
- Work weekdays
- Work weekends

Robert
Check (✓):
- Use a computer
- Answer the phone
- Organize files
- Speak Spanish
- Help people
- Work weekdays

Page 142, Exercise C

Answers will vary.

Page 143, Exercise A

1. Were / was
2. Was / wasn't
3. Were / were
4. Were / weren't
5. Was / was
6. were
7. was
8. were
9. was / was
10. was / was

Page 143, Exercise B

1. Were your parents in Colombia last year?
2. How long was she a caregiver?
3. Were they in school yesterday?
4. Was Ms. Robles sick last week?
5. Were you a nurse in that hospital?
6. Was his job full-time?

Page 144, Exercise C

Joe: (office assistant) Were you an office assistant at Medici Accounting?
Hai: Yes, I was.
Joe: How long were you there?
Hai: Two years.
Joe: (job duties) What were your job duties?
Hai: Answering the phone, taking messages, making copies, and organizing files.
Joe: Were you an office assistant at Greyhound Computers also?
Hai: Yes, I was.
Joe: How long were you there?
Hai: Nine months.
Joe: (job duties) What were your job duties?
Hai: Answering the phone, taking messages, and organizing files.

Page 145

Answers will vary.

Audio CD Track List

		Track
Audio Introduction		1
Unit 1		
Page 5	Exercise E	2
Page 6	Exercise A	3
Page 6	Exercise B	4
Page 11	Exercise A	5
Page 13	Exercise E	6
Unit 2		
Page 17	Exercise D	7
Page 18	Exercise A	8
Page 18	Exercise C	9
Page 19	Exercise E	10
Page 19	Exercise F	11
Page 22	Exercise C	12
Page 23	Exercise A	13
Page 24	Exercise C	14
Page 25	Exercise F	15
Unit 3		
Page 31	Exercise A	16
Page 33	Exercise D	17
Page 34	Exercise C	18
Page 36	Exercise B	19
Page 37	Exercise F	20
Unit 4		
Page 41	Exercise F	21
Page 42	Exercise A	22
Page 44	Exercise F	23
Page 45	Exercise A	24
Page 46	Exercise D	25
Page 47	Exercise B	26
Page 48	Exercise F	27
Unit 5		
Page 55	Exercise F	28
Page 58	Exercise D	29
Page 59	Exercise A	30

		Track
Unit 6		
Page 65	Exercise C	31
Page 66	Exercise A	32
Page 69	Exercise A	33
Page 70	Exercise E	34
Page 73	Exercise D	35
Unit 7		
Page 78	Exercise A	36
Page 83	Exercise A	37
Page 85	Exercise B	38
Unit 8		
Page 91	Exercise A	39
Page 93	Exercise D	40
Page 95	Exercise C	41
Page 97	Exercise C	42
Unit 9		
Page 103	Exercise B	43
Page 106	Exercise D	44
Page 107	Exercise A	45
Page 109	Exercise C	46
Unit 10		
Page 116	Exercise B	47
Page 117	Exercise D	48
Page 119	Exercise A	49
Page 121	Exercise D	50
Unit 11		
Page 126	Exercise A	51
Page 129	Exercise A	52
Page 131	Exercise A	53
Page 132	Exercise A	54
Page 132	Exercise C	55
Unit 12		
Page 136	Exercise B	56
Page 138	Exercise A	57
Page 141	Exercise D	58
Page 142	Exercise A	59